Purchased Innocence

A Transformation from Victim to Victor

R. MICHELLE LAZOS

Copyright © 2020 by Michelle Lazos

All rights reserved. No part of this publication may be reproduced, distributed, or transmitted in any form or by any means, including photocopying, recording, or other electronic or mechanical methods, without the prior written permission of the author, except in the case of brief quotations embodied in critical reviews and certain other noncommercial uses permitted by copyright law. For permission requests, contact the author.

All scripture, unless otherwise indicated is taken from the New King James Version.
Scripture taken from the New King James Version®. Copyright © 1982 by Thomas Nelson. Used by permission. All rights reserved.

Scripture quotations marked (AMP) are taken from the Amplified Bible, Copyright © 1954, 1958, 1962, 1964, 1965, 1987 by The Lockman Foundation. Used by permission.

Scriptures marked KJV are taken from the KING JAMES VERSION (KJV): KING JAMES VERSION, public domain.

First edition 2020

Print ISBN: 978-0-9993807-6-5
eBook ISBN: 978-0-9993807-7-2

Some names and identifying details have been changed to protect the privacy of individuals.

Printed in the United States of America

This book is dedicated to my Lord and Savior Jesus Christ, whose mercy and love found me in the depths of despair; to my children Aja & Isaiah who have responded to me with love and forgiveness; to my mama and dad who stepped in to raise my children; to my brothers who put up with a lot from me and still tried to love me; and to every brother and sister in Christ who kept me covered in prayer so that this God-given assignment could be birthed.

All glory, honor, and praise to Jesus Christ, my Lord and Savior.

Contents

Preface 7
Chapter I 11
Chapter II 14
Chapter III 23
Chapter IV 33
Chapter V 37
Chapter VI 41
Chapter VII 44
Chapter VIII 47
Chapter IX 51
Chapter X 58
Chapter XI 62
Chapter XII 65
Chapter XIII 68
Chapter XIV 71

Chapter XV	76
Chapter XVI	81
Chapter XVII	88
Chapter XVIII	92
Chapter XIX	101
Chapter XX	105
Chapter XXI	113
Chapter XXII	118
Chapter XXIII	123
Chapter XXIV	127
Chapter XXV	132
Chapter XXVI	135
Chapter XXVII	138
Reflection	147
Resources	151
Resource Links	153
Identity in Christ	155
Morning Protection Prayer	157
Prayer of Declarations & Decrees from Spiritual & Physical Imprisonment	163
Additional Information	173

Preface

As I was ministering in a women's prison in Texas, I heard the Holy Spirit whisper, "Purchased Innocence." I knew immediately it was the title of the book about my life. He was in fact, at that moment, commissioning me to put the life of pain I had endured into a book. Two days after hearing the title of the book, the Holy Spirit fell on me and produced a thirty-page outline of what would become the book, in two and a half hours, which was written by hand.

I went on to give the written testimony in Houston, Texas where it was confirmed I was called to write a book. I was excited yet scared, because I did not want to reveal the identity of someone whom God had led me to forgive for abusing me when I was a kid. I began praying to God asking Him for wisdom so that I could write the book. He spoke to my heart, "Love covers a multitude of sins and your testimony won't be built on the backs of those who have hurt you, but on Me!" The Holy Spirit began ministering to me and telling me that my focus had always been on what was done to me and what Satan stole from me, but He wants me to focus on what Jesus purchased for me with His own precious blood.

There was a great exchange that took place when the Holy Spirit got ahold of my heart and began to birth compassion, mercy, love, and forgiveness for those who hurt me. I always planned to write a book and in addition to the name being changed from Stolen Innocence to Purchased Innocence, there was also an exchange evident in the meaning behind my book cover. Two years before this encounter with the Holy Spirit I had stumbled on this red handprint on google images. At this time, I was still bitter and angry and planned to write a book to expose everyone that hurt me in life. I can now see I wore the identity of a victim. Originally, I visualized this red handprint being in finger-paint to symbolize the innocence of childhood and to symbolize the memories that seemed to be etched so deep in my soul, that it kept me bound in that time and at that age. Well, that all changed the moment I was given the name *Purchased Innocence* as the Holy Spirit began to minister the new meaning of that same handprint. He spoke to my heart that the red paint now signifies His blood and the handprint is the identifying mark of the "new" man, much like a fingerprint, that proved that by His blood I was purchased, and my identity is now found in Him. It was the manifestation of going from victim to victor. "But thanks be to God, who gives us the victory through our Lord Jesus Christ (1 Corinthians 15:57)."

I'm depending on the Holy Spirit to write everything He intends to be written through me, as His surrendered vessel. It's important to me that the words He gave me are not altered in anyway. I pray that my testimony gives you hope, and I want you to know that despite every dark struggle you have endured, you are dearly loved by God the Father and His precious Son, Jesus Christ and through the power of His Holy Spirit you can overcome sin and darkness and be renewed and transformed into the image of His dear Son, Jesus Christ. I pray you never forget that Jesus purchased you with His own blood to redeem you from the hands of Satan. In Jesus there is fullness of life, for He is the Way, the Truth, and the Life and no one can come to the Father except through Him (John 14:6).

My testimony centers on the power of forgiveness and how receiving the love of Jesus Christ enabled me to forgive those who have hurt me and to receive forgiveness for my own sins. In order for God's glory to be shown, I have to go over my history, so that you may grasp the level of darkness Jesus Christ rescued me from and to prove to you there is no depth that is too deep for the hand of Jesus to reach. I will also share revelations given to me by the Holy Spirit with hopes it will help you just as it has helped me.

Chapter I

*"Before I formed you in the womb I knew you;
Before you were born I sanctified you; I ordained
you a prophet to the nations." – Jeremiah 1:5*

My name is Rebecca Michelle Lazos, I was named after my mom, so I have always been called Michelle. My paternal grandmother is from Mexico, and she often called me Micha, which is short for Michaela (the Spanish version of Michelle). Most people know me by Michelle, but those closest to me call me Micha. I was born on March 1, 1985 in a tiny west Texas town called Denver City. I was the second child born to my parents, who are still married today. My dad is Mexican, and my mom is German. I have an older brother who is named after my dad, Oscar Michael, but we call him Mike since my dad goes by his first name. Mike and I are only a year apart, but I also have a younger brother named Maxx, who is eight years younger.

Mike and I were so close, and we are even the same age for eight days every year. I loved to call us twins when we were little, but as the big brother it would make him mad, and he would tell me to stop saying that. Mike and

I were very dependent on each other, especially during the times our dad would drink too much. Our dad was a severe alcoholic and our house was full of fear and anxiety. Don't get me wrong my dad has some great qualities and I love spending time with him, but the effects of alcoholism seemed to overshadow many of his good attributes while I was growing up. My dad comes from a long line of musicians and music was always a big part of our lives. He played rock, blues and Tejano music. However, usually when there was music, there was also alcohol. As a child I began to associate music and alcohol together. Music would act as a warning of what may be expected later. I understand now, after struggling in addiction, that parents often have unresolved trauma, which make it impossible for them to be the parents their children deserve. It's not a good excuse, but it is a valid one. Regardless, we all must be accountable for the choices we make and the way they affect others.

 I loved to spend time listening to my dad play the guitar and would watch his fingers intently as he strummed or picked at the strings. We had a lot of great times and memories and I'm thankful to God that my dad always protected me to the best of his ability. My mother always had a job, usually more than one, and looking back I can see she did the best she could as well. My mother would go on to become a teacher and do her best to provide everything we needed. My mom lavished love on us, and we always felt safe with her. She was in no way perfect, but she was the only stability we had as children. My mom never let us know how poor we were, and we never missed having a birthday party or Christmas presents. She always found a way to make it happen and was involved in school functions whenever she could. Sometimes, my dad would come too, and this would always make me happy. My dad would play baseball with us and take us on his boat or to the beach. He was not a bad dad at all, but the effects of alcohol would steal him away. Who he was in the beginning of the day, wasn't who he ended up being later that night.

Chapter II

*"The thief does not come except to steal,
and to kill, and to destroy. I have come that
they may have life, and that they may have
it more abundantly." – John 10:10*

Although my dad protected me the best he could, he wasn't always present to do that. When I was about four years old, I was at my grandpa's house playing outside with a group of boys that lived next door. The next thing I knew my little body was laying in the wagon and they had my legs propped up on the sides while they all looked and took turns touching me. I remember that I felt like I was outside of my body looking down on what was happening. I learned later in life this is called disassociating. I can remember to this day where everyone was standing. For many years I repressed that memory, but at some point, it came forth and I can remember every detail. This seemed to mark me with an invitation for abuse for the rest of my life.

Nobody ever found out, and soon after, we moved to Florida. A major reason we moved to Florida was because of my Grammy, my mom's mother. She lived in Florida and my parents needed her support. We moved right up the street from her. She was a huge part of my life and we were very close. She was a huge help to my mom both financially and taking care of me and my brothers. She was always close, so she would pick me and my brother up from school or watch us when my mom was working two jobs and my dad wasn't around because of work or alcohol. My mom always said she didn't figure my dad into the daily equation because he wasn't dependable. If he was there to help... great, but she always had a backup which was Grammy. As I got older, she always took me shopping, to nice restaurants, dancing, and even to Cancun, Mexico. I loved her so much and she meant the world to me.

When we got to Florida, I remember walking into a
K-mart and as my mom held open the door for me, in excitement and hopefulness I said, "I can't wait to die!"

She sternly responded, "Don't say that!"

I responded in confusion and innocence, "What? I want to go back with Jesus."

I'm not exactly sure how I knew how much I loved Jesus then. My dad was raised Catholic and my mom was raised Baptist. My mom's grandparents were Pentecostal, but I somehow was never raised in church. Despite not being raised in church, I was raised with my mom praying with us. We would always pray on the way to school and she would talk about Jesus, but we never as a family read the Bible. We would go to church here and there, but it was never more than a couple times every few years.

I also remember laying at my dad's feet as he would watch TV and I felt complete peace. I didn't understand it until recently when I was worshiping God, bowed over in His presence, envisioning laying at the Father's feet, that I realized my spirit man, even as a child yearned to be with God the Father and in His presence.

When I was five years old and waiting to begin Kindergarten, I often would go to Mike's class when my mom would volunteer at his school. I remember learning about fire safety from a fireman named Towtruck. One day my parents were at work, and Mike and I were with our babysitter. I began smelling a strong odor and my brother began coughing a lot. Although we couldn't see any smoke, I knew something was terribly wrong. I kept telling the babysitter something was wrong, but she ignored me and began spraying Obsession cologne everywhere, which made Mike cough more. I was worried about my brother because of his severe asthma. I began telling them it's a sign of a fire, but nobody would listen. In an instant I was quickened with great wisdom for a five-year-old. I saw she wasn't going to leave, so I decided to suggest us going outside to play Duck-Duck-Goose. Both the babysitter and my brother said no, so I decided to suggest candy and beef jerky from the store down the street, and they both agreed with excitement. The entire time we walked I understood what I did only to a certain extent. As we walked back, we began seeing tons of smoke swirling around the cul- de-sac and to the tops of the palm trees. I began saying, "I told you so! I told you our house was on fire!"

When we arrived at our apartment there were firetrucks and our neighbors had been yelling for us. They all thought we were inside and were perhaps trying to wake my father. They had no idea how God gave me a plan to save us from harm. I know the fire safety helped, but I remember the moment divine wisdom was initiated from the Holy Spirit. I felt it with a physical force, and the confidence and boldness

I had was not of me. It was determined the cause of fire was a rag that she used to heat tortillas. The babysitter soaked it in water, then wrapped it in newspaper and placed it in the trash beneath a ton of chemicals, which made it smolder and then ignite. She was only sixteen and was scared to be in trouble. We had to move into my grandma's while our apartment was repaired. It mostly stayed in the kitchen, but our clothes were ruined from smoke damage and the silver wheels of my '57 Chevy Barbie car turned yellow. I will never forget that day and I am thankful for the Holy Spirit leading us to safety.

When Kindergarten started, I remember this Jewish girl in my class said that Jesus isn't the Son of God. It felt like someone had punched me in my stomach and ripped out my heart. I felt like I wanted to hit her and cry at the same time. I just responded loudly, "Jesus is the Son of God!" Looking back on my life I can see how God was always with me, carefully leading me with His eye upon me. I may not have yet been born-again, but He was making sure I had the opportunity.

When I was in first grade my relationship with Mike began to change. I was very protective of him even though he was older. Mike was bullied by a boy at school, and I later found out that the same boy who bullied him, gave him his phone number. This angered me because I didn't want him being friends with somebody who treated him that way, so I took the number and tore it up. In return, this made Mike very angry and he punched me in my nose and broke it. We were with the babysitter, but neither the babysitter, nor my parents deemed it necessary to seek medical attention for my nose, so I went through most of my life without being able to breathe out of one nostril.

Later that year, my dad's friend was over, and during his visit, he tried to get me to go to bed. He said, "Come on, go to bed and I will read you a killer bedtime story." My dad was working at a sporting goods store and this guy was his coworker. His friend told me he was also a gymnastics coach, but I didn't believe him. I thought he was lying in an attempt to connect with me because I was taking gymnastics. I knew there was something wrong with him. I refused to go to my room and stuck near my dad. I don't think my dad heard him because the music was loud, and he whispered near my ear. Even though my dad wasn't present to protect me all the time, this was one of those times I relied on him as my protector and he made me feel safe.

However, there were times when I felt alone and had to fend for myself. When I turned eight years old, a close family friend would be at my house a lot. He molested me over and over. It continued throughout my childhood, but I never told anyone. I continued to have good behavior, but I was dying inside. Looking back at the pictures of myself, I wonder how on Earth nobody knew. I looked like I had no soul and any remnants had been broken into tiny pieces. As a coping mechanism, I was in complete denial of being a girl and even needing a bra. I developed very fast for my age and my mom and dad would give me bras for presents. I remember one day around the fourth grade being given a backpack. Inside the backpack were new bras. Most girls couldn't wait for this time in their life, but I threw them and screamed at the top of my lungs! I hated everything about being a girl, including the attention. I was expressing and reacting to the molestation through the hate of being a girl. I hated what attracted abuse to me. I finally told my best friend when I was eleven years old, and she became the person I confided in about it.

Aside from this, I had a fairly normal childhood and a few good friends. However, I learned some of my friend's parents had a problem with my dad being Mexican. This caused me to be rejected a lot or talked about at school. Some of my friends that I wanted to hang out with weren't allowed to come over to my house because my dad was Mexican. I had a few good friends though throughout elementary school, and we often stayed the night at each other's houses. There were times people would bad mouth Mexicans in front of me not knowing I too was Mexican because I looked white. I was only in elementary school, and it hurt a lot for people to say bad things like racial slurs about my dad. I was very proud of my dad and proud that he played music and spoke Spanish. I continued to feel this rejection even by other Latino people, because I discovered there is a hierarchy of Latinos, in which Mexicans were at the bottom. This ideology was very prominent in south Florida. Looking back, I can see how desperate people were to exalt themselves above each other, because of their own pride and inferiority. Most of all my friends were wealthy, and I clearly didn't belong in the group of friends I had. I felt so broken down. I couldn't connect to other kids. I was trying my best to fit in but was constantly being rejected. On top of being rejected, kids were going on with their kid lives and I couldn't because my innocence was taken. I felt like no one cared. This is when my obsession with death began. This obsession would grow powerfully over the coming years.

In fifth grade, my parents separated because of my dad's drinking. He moved back to Texas and we stayed in Florida. I felt sad to lose my protector but also confused because he started dating another woman. At the same time, I also felt relief to not have him and my mom fighting. My mom also began dating someone else and that made me very angry. I didn't like to see my mom with anyone else. The man she was seeing had a son. One day, I am not sure why, but we were both left alone. He was several years older than me and at least 6'4 with very broad shoulders. He began talking to me differently than the other times I had seen him. It wasn't so much what he said but the eerie feeling I felt when he spoke. At the time I didn't have a bedroom and slept in an unairconditioned room known as a "Florida room." It had jalousie windows that had to be cranked in order to open. Since I didn't have a room, I went into my brother's room and put a dresser in front of it so he would not come in. He tried to come in and asked me to come out, but I just stayed in the room. I knew he was trying to molest me. I felt it like a thick presence. This left me feeling scared without my dad to be my protector.

Not only did I have to deal with added stressors, I was still being exposed to the family friend who was still molesting me all these years later. I was telling my best friend on the phone one day that the molestation happened again. This time her mom happened to be listening in on the phone call and overheard me. This was before the time of cell phones when we only had landlines, and often people would quietly pick up another phone in the house and eavesdrop on the call. I think a part of me wished it would have never been heard. Until this point, I didn't really have to deal with what was happening and continued being in denial. However, her mom told my mom and my whole world came crashing down. In the beginning I was hopeful to be removed from the home and be allowed to go live up the street with my grandmother, but that was short-lived.

I wasn't removed from the home and my mother didn't handle the situation. Rage and PTSD took over. My mom basically did nothing with the information because when the information came to light, the abuse stopped. The effects of PTSD came full-force and my behavior seemed to change overnight. One of the symptoms of PTSD is sensory overload and distorted perception. I would often see myself walking in front of myself and objects changing, like doorknobs and stairs. I would go to reach for a doorknob, and it would be much further away or go to step on the stairs and nearly fall because the stair was further down than I thought. This began a twenty-year journey of living in constant sensory overload. My mom never told my dad what was going on when she found out about the abuse, and I didn't either.

Seeing my dad react with violence and be volatile towards my mother my whole life, aided in the way I responded to my rage. I mimicked what I saw and lashed out at whoever was closest. The burden of the molestation was too much to carry. The level of rage that came over me still scares me to this day. I remember chasing Mike with tennis rackets and trying to stab him. I would sit behind the couch with a knife trying to stab him in his back. I hate that I terrorized him that way. Rage would be one of the largest hurdles I'd ever have to overcome and caused me the most difficulty, especially legally and physically. Scripture says, "Whoever has no rule over his own spirit is like a city broken down, without walls" (Proverbs 25:28). I wish I would've at least read the book of Proverbs as a child. I was the epitome of the foolish man and adulteress woman spoken of in Proverbs. It's no coincidence when I began walking in obedience to God, this was the first book of the Bible I began reading with my children.

Jesus says, "The thief does not come except to steal, and to kill, and to destroy. I have come that they may have life, and that they may have it more abundantly" (John 10:10). I can clearly see the first thing Satan did was steal from me. He stole my innocence. He had no hope of killing or destroying me until he had stolen from me. Therefore, he aims to move through others to abuse children. I used to be obsessed with what Satan stole.

Chapter III

Whoever has no rule over his own spirit Is like a city broken down, without walls. - Proverbs 25:28

By the time I was twelve, I began smoking cigarettes and marijuana, running away, and my rage was becoming increasingly violent. My mom started going to church and taking us with her, but I was so consumed in my trauma that I had no interest in attending. My relationship with God consisted of my mom praying with us. When I was in sixth grade, I told a fellow classmate that I wanted to commit suicide, so she provided me what was supposedly horse tranquilizers. I remember they were huge pills, but never knew if it was true or not. I attempted suicide for the first time by overdosing on those pills. I still don't understand why my classmate gave them to me knowing I was going to commit suicide. I remember viewing my body from above and was completely aware I was dead or dying, but I was very happy about it. I went into a black tunnel and saw images of my family flashing by, but I still didn't want to live. I then saw the image of my baby brother Maxx, who was about two years old at the time. Since I was no stranger to prayer, I began pleading with God to let me come back because I couldn't leave him.

God let me come back and I woke up blind and deaf. I remember immediately needing to throw up and groping my way to the bathroom. I was blind for only a short time, but I was deaf for several days. I had already been suspended from school for ten days for fighting, so I didn't have to deal with school while being deaf. My mom would come into my room and tell me she was leaving for work and I would acknowledge her, but never told her I couldn't hear or that I had attempted suicide. I was scared that I would be in trouble, so I never told her until many years later.

I promised God I would never do it again and told Him I was sorry, but not too long after, I'd do it again. I told my mom that time and she took me to the hospital to drink charcoal. I don't know why I told her that time but not the previous time that I actually died. I became so obsessed with death. I would hang live roses upside down on my bedroom wall and would enjoy watching them die. It was like it was a visual representation of my hardened soul; each layer wilting away until only dark and dry segments remained. I would meticulously plan my funeral and often drift away into mesmerizing daydreams of funeral processions and visualizing myself in a casket. The false peace I felt when seeing myself in a casket was overwhelming. They say sleep is the cousin of death and I would have to agree because I realized if I couldn't die, then I'd just sleep. I covered my windows with foil and slept as much as possible. The spirit of suicide continued to follow me.

One day, we went to the daycare to pick up my little brother Maxx, and my mom saw a man there with a corvette. She made a comment about dating him and I got angry. I made fun of him for being bald because my dad was never bald, and she back handed me in my mouth. I was so hurt that she hit me because she never hit me. I didn't understand why she would do this to me over a man she didn't even know. When we got home, I picked up Maxx's plastic baseball bat and started saying, "Hey batta-batta," pretending I was going to hit her. It made me feel good to see her scared after what she did to me. I was honestly holding so much in from years of abuse and trauma. She called the police on me and they forced me to go to a mental hospital. I think my mom thought she was punishing me, but I learned while I was at the hospital that if you say you're going to commit suicide in Florida, then the police must take you to a mental hospital.

This new information I learned meant I could now legally leave my house. I began saying I would commit suicide and they would send me to a mental hospital while I was only in sixth grade. These places became a refuge for me. I'd find peace and solace in these hospitals. I would often have no symptoms after arriving, so they couldn't keep me more than a week, then I would return home. This is also where I received the diagnosis of bi-polar disorder and was placed on medication. My rage continued, so I continued getting in trouble for fighting at school. I was about to throw a girl down the gym bleachers one day when I heard a voice say, "Don't do that! You'll kill her!" So, instead I threw her down in between the bleacher seats and stomped her. I'm not proud of what I did, but I'm thankful God intervened. This was my first encounter with the voice of God.

I left the middle school I was attending and went to the school where my mom taught. I got in even more trouble there and was put in drop-out prevention. I hated school because I hated people. I would ask to be put in In-School

Suspension (ISS) and while I was there, I did my schoolwork, and I was never a problem. I always loved to learn, but I was just emotionally traumatized. I had trouble interacting with students and had the emotional maturity of a young child, so when I was alone I did better. I eventually went to an alternative school and it was awful because none of these kids wanted to learn, but I did. There was no structure, and all the students were just baby sat. I wasn't used to not learning at all. I often skipped school or would purposely not wear my uniform so they would send me home on the city bus. I'd take it to go hangout on the streets and not come back to school, but my mom was never aware of what I was doing. I also started running away, on top of attending an alternative school, constant suspension, and when I wasn't suspended, skipping school. Whenever I would run away, my mom would always come looking for me. She had a way of getting the right information and paying the right people to find out where I was.

When I got to seventh grade, I think my behavior contributed to my parents reconciling because typically my dad could always get us to behave. My dad moved back to Florida with us, and we went to pick him up at the airport as a family. We were very happy to see him and things seemed to get better with my parents. Although things seemed to be changing, one thing that remained the same was my dad's drinking. However, we did get to move out of that small house and into a house with a nice pool. I even had a bedroom that led out to the pool. Whenever I'd run away, my dad often said to me that he didn't understand why I was doing it seeing that he got us a pool. He didn't know all that had happened when he was gone, and I felt I couldn't tell him for fear he'd hurt the people responsible.

I met a girl named Mary and we became best friends. She lived in my grandma's apartment complex, and her mom gave us little to no supervision. Mary's mom would have me drive this car. This car could be driven and dropped off all throughout the hood and it didn't require a key to start it. I soon found out it was a stolen car, but even after learning it was stolen, I continued to be reckless and drove it. I was never caught by the police, but I remember my mom found me standing next to it during one of her runaway searches, and I had to go home. I also started stealing my parent's car at night. Not only was I stealing their car, I stole mom's ATM card and took a couple hundred dollars from her account. I spent it on getting my nails done, and my friend's nails done. When my mom found out, she was furious, and she had every right to be. She shed tears about how careless I was and how hard she worked to give us a good life. Part of me felt remorseful, but the other part didn't care because nobody cared how I was hurting. My dad was still drinking heavily and was mostly uninvolved. I became so careless that I did not fear punishment. The worst thing anybody could do to me was kill me and that would be doing me a favor. I didn't care how I hurt my mom or how hard my mom worked for her money, because I constantly viewed myself as the victim. During this time my mom worked full-time as a teacher and waited tables at night. I also wanted to be accepted by others and would do stupid things for them, and I was addicted to the high of danger. I can understand why people thought I was a drug addict at this time, I disappeared for long periods of time and stole money and forged stolen checks.

On one occasion I decided I was going to run away. I skipped school that day with my friend Alana and we were at my house. She was one of my mom's students and was my partner in crime toward the end of my middle school years. I don't remember how we got a ride, but we picked up someone she referred to as her sister, so that we could get a hotel room paid for. Her sister's boyfriend was from central America and had a lot of money. We got situated in our hotel and Alana called one of her boyfriends over that belonged to a particular gang. He came over and we all went swimming, but then she went upstairs and called her other boyfriend over who was in a rival gang of the boyfriend that was already present. I was yelling at her, "What are you doing!" I was angry she was being so reckless and seemed to be setting them both up to be killed. I still never understood her reason for doing that.

The next thing we knew, there were two rival gangs in the parking lot going back and forth with threats and each of them trying to one up each other in the size of their weapons. We were headed for one of their cars, but at that moment, the guy who got us the room had someone get out of his car with a bazooka over his shoulder pointing it at the other car. So, we decided to run toward the car with the bigger weapon and ride with them. We all took off from the parking lot and the same guy who got us the room the first time got us another hotel room somewhere else. We ended up separating from Alana's sister because she and her boyfriend were going to Miami, so we tried to find other places to stay. We ended up staying at a Cuban family's house until one evening Alana asked to use the pay phone to call one of her boyfriends. I kept yelling at her to get off the phone. I knew with all my being she was being held up with conversation on the phone so both of our moms could find us. In a matter of minutes, it was proven he was working with our moms. My mom pulled up with Alana's mom and we took off on a high-speed chase.

I eventually told the guy driving to stop because I knew my mom was not going to give up and I didn't want any of us getting killed. I got out of the car and Alana's mom dragged her out by her hair.

Anytime Alana and I were caught running away we would just go home and regroup with another plan. I remember one time we skipped school and we took a cab to our middle school, which is where my mom worked as a teacher, and stole her car while she was teaching. When she walked out after a long day, her car was gone. I believe she knew it was me right away. I ran away so often and stole the car so often that all the events seem to run together at times. I know I am so sorry for the embarrassment I caused my mom in front of her friends and colleagues and the constant fear of me dying she lived in.

Being raised during the gangsta rap generation contributed to my mentality and I now see how Satan used music to destroy my young mind, just as he continues to do today. When I was growing up, the street life was glamourized, and murder and violence seemed to be romanticized. I was not from the hood, but as a young girl that's where I was drawn. I do acknowledge part of that fanaticism was also attaching myself to the black race, because that was the only race I was exposed to that hadn't abused me as a child. Prior to the childhood abuse coming out I was attracted to all races of people, but once the identity of someone who molested me as a kid was brought into the open, I could no longer stand the sight of white people. This is coming from a girl who looks mostly white. Some recognize I'm of Hispanic ethnicity, but most do not see me and think, "She's Mexican." It would take many years before I was willing to forgive the people who inflicted great levels of grief and trauma on me.

If I would have understood what unforgiveness did, and the life I would suffer in the years to come, I would have forgiven all my transgressors that day!

I remember one night in eighth grade, I snuck out of my house to go hang out with these guys. It was the night before Easter, and they were dope dealers and older than me. They traded some crack to some people in exchange for their apartment. A friend of mine was with the older guy in the living room and I was in the bedroom using cocaine with the younger guy. At one point I got mad and threw the cocaine on the floor. I had no addiction to this stuff yet and didn't understand how much it cost either. As I was standing there, I heard the front door get kicked in and people yelling. I thought it was the cops, so I hid in the closet. I waited for it to get quiet before I came out. When I came out there was blood everywhere. Apparently, the apartment owners came back after they ran out of crack and kicked their own apartment door in so that they could rob the dope dealer. They held my friend at knife point and stabbed the guy my friend was with in the living room. The apartment owners took the crack and ran. Once me and the younger guy came in the living room and saw what happened, we all ran out of there. The two dope dealers went one way, still injured, and my friend and I walked the other direction.

Even though I was living recklessly, I knew there was a place deep within me that had been hardened and covered with pain; a place that desired to know my Creator. I found an old Children's Bedtime Bible that my grandma gave me with black and white illustrations. It was divided into 365 days and took you through the major stories in the Bible. I wrote a message to the guy I was doing cocaine with that read, "I read this book and it really helped me and I know it will help you too." I never had a chance to give it to him.

On another occasion, my friend Alana was staying in a beautiful condo on the beach. I went to take her some clothes because she was a runaway. It was so beautiful, and I didn't want to miss out on any fun, so I decided to stay with her. There were at least three grown men in their mid-twenties who were staying there, and they were selling crack to this lady who owned both the condo we were staying in and the condo next door where she was staying. She stayed in one smoking crack while we stayed in the other condo next to her. During this time, one of the guys asked if I wanted to be a getaway driver for a bank robbery. I replied to him, "No, I'm not going to take part in a bank robbery." I do not think I believed they were really going to do it, but I also didn't know one of them was wanted for a bank robbery in Atlanta.

After a few days, the lady who owned both condos got angry because she wanted more dope, so she called the police on the dealers. Two of them ran and one of them jumped off the balcony onto the sandy beach. Alana and I were interrogated by the police. They eventually let us go, but insisted we had to leave. We left and went to another nearby city where I would later get so sick that I had to be dropped off at a hospital and was forced to call my mom so they would treat me. I had excruciating headaches, fever, and was even vomiting neon green. This would happen to me often when I would run away. I would end up extremely sick with random illnesses and have no choice but to go home. When I got home the news came on to report a bank robbery in downtown. Before they named the suspects or showed their pictures, I said two of their names. My mom's mouth dropped, and she asked how I knew who they were. I told her that they asked me to be the getaway driver. I enjoyed shocking my mom, but I did not realize the magnitude of the situation.

Chapter IV

*"Let all bitterness, wrath, anger, clamor,
and evil speaking be put away from you,
with all malice." – Ephesians 4:31*

When I was fourteen, I started high-school and was in the self-contained class because of my behavior.

I remember they wouldn't let me walk around without a security escort because I would fight. I would make a reason up in my mind to fight and make myself believe it, then go hit someone. I ended up fighting a big football player and got my head kicked in very badly. I never expected to win, but I was tired of him taunting me and I needed to release all the anger and rage that was accumulating over the years. The truth is I would find any reason to fight anyone, and many of them were guys. Since the sixth grade it was common for me to return after a ten-day suspension only to be on another suspension within a few hours.

I ran away one day and was hanging out at this woman's apartment in the projects. Since I ran away a lot, I spent a lot of time downtown and she was always around. She was an adult and had two small children. Most of the time I ran away just to be away from home. I wasn't out getting drunk or high on hard drugs. I smoked weed and did cocaine sometimes, but only when it was around me. I hadn't yet reached that level of addiction. My biggest addiction was looking for acceptance in the wrong places and being naive to how the world works, especially the streets. This guy named Cash was at her house and he kept trying to get with me, but I wouldn't entertain him because I wasn't interested. I ended up leaving to walk to the store and he followed me. As we were walking, he asked if he could buy me anything. I told him no, because I knew he would try to use that as a reason I had to return a "favor." We went into the store and I bought what I wanted, and we left. Cash suggested we go to his brother's house to get weed. I asked him where he lived, and he told me. I knew of his brother and what house he was referring to, so we walked there.

There were two guys at his brother's house, and they were watching that movie *Life* with Eddie Murphy. I still can't stand that movie to be played. I asked Cash for a cigarette and he told me that they were in the room on the dresser. I walked in there alone and I can't remember if I got one, because the next thing I knew I was face down on a bed and my head was being pushed into a pillow. I couldn't breathe. Cash began to sodomize me, and I remember feeling the greatest pain I ever felt. I have no doubt an angel was with me because I somehow got him off me. I bucked him off me like I was a bull. He was a grown man, at least twenty-five years old, and I was fourteen years old and under 125 pounds. I began throwing my clothes on and cussing him out. I overheard the two men in the other room while I was fighting Cash and cussing him out, that they had "taken a ride" to feed white girls to the gators. I knew whenever someone said "take a ride" that meant that person was not coming back. It then occurred to me that this man could kill me. I instantly changed and began pretending to be his girlfriend. I have carried extreme guilt over this, but I have learned what I did was normal and a mode of survival. He then walked me around the hood to different family member's houses as his girlfriend. I wanted to scream but at the same time felt like I was in a movie and none of it was real. Later that evening, we rode the bus to his parent's house in the country where he continued raping and sodomizing me on an abandoned school bus on their property. I guess some would argue that I allowed him, but I know I was terrified and didn't know what to do. I was cooperating out of fear. I remember I had on a maroon high-school shirt with RHS in white lettering on the front left and black shorts. I remember I was very cold and scared. The next day we went to my house. There is no good explanation for why I would bring him there. He took a shower in my bathroom and I went to my mom's shower and cried as I scrubbed and scrubbed my body. I got out of the shower and got dressed. I remember giving him all my gold jewelry even though he didn't ask for it. I don't understand what was going on in my mind. People would see me and call me Cash or refer to me as his girlfriend. I don't know why nobody was worried that I was only fourteen.

  I remember the day I told my mom what happened to me. I don't even think I planned to tell my mom, but I was forced to because I was scared Cash had given me AIDS. He told people he had been with me and they told me I should get checked because he was known to be with prostitutes. I was terrified and depended on my mom to guide me through that scary time. I told her the same thing I typed above, and her response was, "That's what you get for being in the street!" She never hugged me or assured me I would be okay. For many years, Satan would continue to replay this over and over in my mind and create a bigger wedge between me and my mom. This was the issue I had with her since I was in elementary school. She never handled the sexual abuse I endured properly or in a way that was beneficial to me. In all honesty, had the childhood sexual abuse been handled better, I honestly doubt I would have been in the street in the first place, and I never would have crossed paths with Cash. The lack of love in my mom's response fueled an increasing hate for women. My dad also didn't speak well about women and that scarred me as a child into my adult years. My dad never talked to me that way but hearing him talk about women negatively made me think that is what men thought of me too.

Chapter V

"And be kind to one another, tenderhearted, forgiving one another, even as God in Christ forgave you." – Ephesians 4:32

I was always trying to escape my home-life and in ninth grade the court ordered me to a therapeutic program. I didn't know then, but my mom was the one who orchestrated the whole thing. I thought the courts did it because I was getting arrested a lot. I never knew it was my mom pushing them to get me help. I would've been dead or kidnapped had my mom not intervened. I know she loved me no matter what I did because she would go into the bad areas of town with no fear. She would pay people to tell her where I was and put posters of me up at gas stations, and approach anyone on the street.

I'm so sorry I ever inflicted this pain and worry on my mom and dad. There are too many incidents to put in this book. You could magnify what you've read by 100 and you still wouldn't reach the magnitude of what I did to people through my actions. I was responding to pain and hurt in the wrong way, thereby creating pain and hurt for them, continuing the cycle. That's what Satan does; he pulls our strings and has us destroy each other while he sits back laughing. The only way to heal is to forgive! We must forgive so we can be healed, so others can be healed and to stop the vicious cycle.

I loved being in the therapeutic camp. We lived outside in tents made of pine tree limbs and trunks that we cut, skinned, and constructed. It was hot in the summer and freezing in the winter. We had to use an outhouse during the day and use a shared bucket at night, which was disgusting, but the best memories I have are from that place. The love I received from the counselors was exactly what my wounded soul needed. I had an opportunity to swim with dolphins in Key Largo on my fifteenth birthday, canoed for twenty-one days straight on the Suwannee River, and saw lighthouses all along the gulf coast of Florida and Alabama. I made best friends that were like sisters and I'm still in contact with many of them today, including the counselors.

During the time in camp my mom would send me long typed letters regularly. Many of the letters were long beautiful prayers. I would read them out loud as if I was the one praying and I would sense great peace. I remember there were times I would be crying out for my dad's salvation in long billowing cries. I didn't know I was not born-again yet, and I thought if I died that day I would be saved. It would be many years before I learned the true gospel of Jesus Christ, which includes repentance, self-denial, picking up your cross, and following Jesus as His disciple. My nickname at camp was Preacher because during meetings I would always bring up the Bible and I also had crosses hanging around my room. I would continue being called names that spoke to the identity Jesus died to give me, although I had not received my new identity yet. Before leaving the therapeutic camp, I decided to write my mom a letter graphically detailing the rape I endured. I made sure to use the most vulgar language and detailed the assault that took place on my tiny body. I never received the response I was looking for and just continued to suppress all the pain within myself. I think the lack of support was worse than the rape itself and set the stage for how I handled rape in the future.

Every six weeks I got to go home on Friday morning until Sunday afternoon. My brother Mike and I had a love/hate relationship. One minute we were hanging out, the next we were fighting. I knew mostly all his friends, but they were never who I chose to hang around. Even though we were raised around the same groups of people, we now lived in two different worlds. He hung with mostly wealthy white kids and I hung in the streets. Whenever I was able to go home during camp, the only way I could leave the house was to go with him. I'd smoke weed while Mike and his friends would do other drugs.

During this time, I began feeling an unusual light throbbing pain in my arms that later would be diagnosed as Fibromyalgia. It is interesting to note it was the same year I cruelly mistreated a girl in that camp. Her mom suffered from Fibromyalgia. One day she was crying, and I asked her what was wrong, and she said her mom was diagnosed with Fibromyalgia. I had never heard of it, so I asked her in the meanest voice, "Can she die?"

She responded, "No."

I said, "Then what are you crying for?"

I had a hard heart and no doubt sowed exactly what I would end up reaping for the next eighteen years. I don't know if I would have ended up with Fibromyalgia regardless, but when I was finally diagnosed years later, I immediately remembered the day I was so cruel.

    I stayed in that program for sixteen months and fifteen days, which was considered a short stay. Ten days later my family moved back to Texas. I know my family was happy in some ways to move back to Texas, but I know they moved for me. I didn't want to remain in Florida, because of the reputation I had, and I wanted a new start. My mom said, "If we move anywhere, we will move back to Texas," and that is exactly what we did!

Chapter VI

"For there is nothing hidden that will not become evident, nor anything secret that will not be known and come out into the open." – Luke 8:17AMP

We moved to Texas in 2001, and I was excited despite moving to a small town. My Grammy moved back with us because she suffered from an aneurysm and we were going to help take care of her. Towards the end of the program, I stopped smoking. When we got to Texas, I did pretty good for a while but started smoking weed again. I had a very valuable diamond ring from Grammy, and I took it off to wash my hands at school. I accidentally left it laying on the sink and this girl named Briana brought it back to me when she found it. We were friends ever since. She introduced me to her cousin, Ellis. We got along well and really liked spending time together, but it was short lived because when I couldn't get a hold of him, I was informed that he moved away to California.

I was a junior and I decided to move on and start dating a guy named Carlos who was also a junior in high school. I knew something was off one day when I woke up.

I got up and got the oil changed in my mom's car. While I was waiting, I took a pregnancy test in Walmart and it was positive. I started caring again about letting my family down, so I didn't want to tell my mom. I was terrified for her to know. Surprisingly, I got a super loving reaction from my mom and she was very supportive about whatever I wanted to do. Apparently, my mom told my dad because when he came home, he told me congrats. Carlos and I had only been dating a short while, but we were broken up for about a month when I found out I was pregnant. Ellis returned from California and told me that he never moved, he was just visiting family for a couple of weeks, so we were dating. When I told Ellis I was pregnant, he wanted to raise my daughter, but I told him that wasn't right, and I broke up with him. We both knew he wasn't the father because we had never been sexually involved. When I told Carlos, at first, he was skeptical about the paternity because I was dating Ellis. Once Carlos accepted that the baby was his, he quickly became excited and was on board and supportive. We got back together, and I quit smoking weed again, but this time it was because I was pregnant. Carlos moved into my mom's house with me. He was very good to me. We went to parenting classes every week in Austin and we prepared in every way we knew how for our princess.

    I struggled in my relationship with Carlos because if I was with the same person for very long, I would begin screaming and fighting them in my sleep. He didn't understand this. It got to the point I asked him to announce himself before he touched me. This was hard for him especially because we would both be asleep and he would just want to hug me and sleep, but I couldn't handle it. One day I was looking on the Sarasota's Most Wanted website, seeing if anyone I knew from Sarasota was in trouble. I read the government name of the man who sodomized me when I was fourteen. I saw his street name "Cash" in quotations. That was the first time I knew his real identity and how old he was. He was twenty- six years old. I looked at what he was wanted for and it was for stabbing someone in the neck, which made me thankful and surprised that I wasn't killed. It amazes me how he told people he had been with me knowing what he did to me, and I was only fourteen at the time.

Chapter VII

*"Every good gift and every perfect gift is
from above, and comes down from the Father
of lights, with whom there is no variation
or shadow of turning." – James 1:17*

On September 10, 2002, I gave birth to my daughter, Aja Anais. She was my world, and she was very blessed to have a stable life, considering Carlos and I were both only seventeen. We continued living with my parents and he began working full-time and getting his GED. I stayed in high-school and remained on honor roll and was able to put my daughter in the school-provided daycare. One month after turning eighteen, I got my own small apartment with Carlos and the three of us moved out of my mom's house. I was a senior in high-school and loved being legally out of my parent's house. A couple months after moving into my own apartment, I bumped into Ellis. He told me he was back living in Texas after spending some time in Louisiana. I did my best to stay out of contact with Ellis and his family while I was with Carlos. I wanted to be devoted and loyal to Carlos and my daughter, but the connection I had with Ellis was not easily forgotten. My heart was always with Ellis, so when I ran into him that day buying tacos, I decided to break up with Carlos so Ellis and I could start dating again. I hate how heartless I was and that I had no compassion on Carlos. He was a wonderful dad and a hard worker. I made a bad decision.

I graduated from high school in May 2003 and began college three days later. I did very well the first semester, but I became increasingly distracted in the second semester. Briana and I grew closer and she was always physically there and really supportive. Always being around each other, we grew extremely close. I began using cocaine again and was back to the street mindset. It's true that you can take a person out of the streets, but it's a completely different thing to take the streets out of the person. The battle is in our mind and until our mind is renewed with the word of God, we will continue returning to the chains that have held us in bondage. "And do not be conformed to this world, but be transformed by the renewing of your mind, that you may prove what is that good and acceptable and perfect will of God" (Romans 12:2).

I remained in college, but the unusual light throbbing pain that I started feeling in my arms during camp got progressively worse. The pain spread to my legs and I was in constant pain. My legs had a bluish tint to them, and the pain made it difficult to be on my feet. Whenever I had to be on my feet for long periods of time, I had to constantly switch legs like a flamingo. It felt like I could feel the insides of my muscles and tendons, and the only thing that eased the pain was applying counter pressure directly to the pain. After I was constantly crying, Ellis got concerned and took me to the hospital. I was then diagnosed with Fibromyalgia.

This meant that my senses were extremely amplified. My hearing was affected, but touch was the worst. Certain clothing, fabrics, and sheets magnified what a normal touch would feel like. I had widespread nerve pain all over my body. Whenever I rode in the car, the vibrations made the car ride unbearable.

They didn't know much about the illness at that time, so they gave me a muscle relaxer and sent me home. I was constantly crying and the pain I felt that day in the therapeutic camp, had grown out of control. I would feel sharp stabbing pain, as if icepicks were stabbing me in my face. I can remember driving and having to pull over so my friend could drive. I was not able to hold the gas pedal down. I would increasingly deal with pain and loss of mobility. I couldn't go shopping because walking was unbearable and moving the clothes on the rack was agonizing. Many times, Ellis and I would go to the mall and I would sit, and Ellis would pick out my clothes and show me. I would tell him whether I liked the clothes or not. He was very good at matching, so I usually had no problem. Plus, I dressed like a tomboy most of the time, so it was easy. Fibromyalgia rapidly aged me, and I spent time going to all kinds of doctors, but no one could really help me.

Chapter VIII

"As a dog returns to his own vomit, So a fool repeats his folly." – Proverbs 26:11

Ellis was constantly looking at porn and it angered me. I felt so rejected and disgusted. I didn't stand up for myself much and was incredibly timid. I came across an ad one day by a lawyer from Alabama. He was looking for women to pay $500.00 to take topless pictures. I called him in front of my boyfriend trying to let him see how I felt when he watched porn, but it didn't work. I asked the lawyer, "What do you do with the pictures?"

He said, "It's a hobby."

I replied, "Let's make it a business!"

I began spewing all kinds of lies including false credentials and was very good at it. He sent me a check for several thousand dollars that day to let me know he was serious. He informed me I would receive $300 for every woman that I was able find who agreed to get their picture taken. Before there was social media, we had AOL chatrooms and profiles. I met a friend in the chatroom who lived in Florida and offered him some money. He agreed to drive any girls in his area that we found that were willing to have their picture taken from Florida to Alabama. I also began using AOL to find women and would set up the details and send them to Alabama where the lawyer was. Often times the women would change their minds, but I would still receive the $300. Soliciting the women was a high, and in an instant, I shifted from victim to controller. I felt safe and powerful, my greedy heart married my hate for women and propelled me into a deeper level of darkness. However, at times my conscience would begin to bother me, and I would want to start helping the women. I was torn between light and darkness but chose to remain in darkness. I had to dehumanize the women and make them more of an object. I pictured the women I was soliciting with $300 above their head. My mentality was, "Better them than me," but looking back I wonder why it had to be either of us. Mike and Ellis were friends and hung out a lot. When Mike found out, he was shocked and said, "There's no way a lawyer is sending you this money and you don't have to do anything."

Ellis vouched saying, "Naw, she just gets on the phone and checks come in the mail."

I felt like they were proud of me and I liked finally being in control, or so I thought.

I decided to go back to Florida and visit my old friend Mary who used to live in my grandma's apartment complex and used this lawyer to make the trip happen. I made all kinds of empty promises. He planned to finally meet me in person there, and I was going to direct a photoshoot of women. He paid for my trip expenses and gave me $500 in spending money, plus the standard $300 per woman. I was about twenty years old and felt like I was on top of the world. My daughter was a toddler and stayed with my mom during my two-week trip to Florida. I went back into the darkness that I scarcely escaped a few years earlier. The taste for more money continued and the street life mentality returned stronger than ever before. I was hoping after two weeks, I would get tired of Florida and be thankful I lived in Texas.

Mary "rented" a car by giving the car owner crack. We were riding around with some friends and stopped by this recreation center that was having a party. The parking lot was packed. Apparently, the guy we rented the truck from was reported missing by his family. He had a son who happened to be in the same parking lot as us and recognized his missing dad's truck. He came over to the window with about twenty people and snatched the keys out the ignition. He was demanding to know where his dad was and where we got his dad's truck. We kept trying to explain that we rented it from him for some crack, but he was convinced his dad stopped using. He thought we hurt his dad and stole his truck. He made us get out and he drove off in his dad's truck. We walked to one of our friend's house nearby until we got back to our original location. We eventually went back to the guy and told him his son took his truck from us, but I'm not sure if anything came of it between them.

It seemed like there was constant chaos. Mary's boyfriend was abusive and terrorized her. One night he became angry at Mary which led to a fit of rage. He forced her in the car to "go for a ride" or what I knew to be feeding her to the gators. I refused to go with her because I had my daughter to think about. I was panicked trying to figure out what to do and find somebody to help her. Thankfully, many hours later, Mary came back. In addition to the truck situation and Mary being kidnapped, my trip to Florida was filled with drugs, danger, and more darkness.

Chapter IX

"Do not forget to entertain strangers, for by so doing some have unwittingly entertained angels." – Hebrews 13:2

After returning to Texas, I was increasingly consumed with material things and money. Ellis and I were already selling weed, and after returning from Florida I suggested we start to sell crack. He previously sold crack, so he was familiar with the game and he taught me and showed me the ropes. Ellis began getting his powder from his cousin Briana's boyfriend, so Briana and I started chillin' again. Ellis didn't use drugs, but he did drink. I would ask him if I could get cocaine because he was against anything other than drinking and smoking weed. I had been doing cocaine heavily for the two weeks I was back in Florida and now felt I had to have it! He hated that I did cocaine, but would let me get a twenty, without giving me a hard time. A twenty is about .20 of a gram. You could get several uses out of that amount if it was used in moderation. Ideally, I liked to do most at once, but I tried not to be excessive. By this time, I was getting addicted to it and wanted more, so by the time my daughter was nearly three years old, I kicked Ellis out so I could freely use.

After he left, he stopped by one day and caught a guy at my house. While I was trying to close the door, Ellis grabbed me by my hair and pulled my head into the door and started slamming the door on my head. Briana was there and called the cops. She wrote a statement and got Ellis sent to jail. Eventually, I dropped the charges against him. I felt bad because I was still allowing him to take care of my daughter and treat her as his own. His whole family treated my daughter as their own. When he got out, he left and went straight to Louisiana.

I began spending a lot of time in Austin at Mike's house. I was approached by a company called Vivid Video, which was part of the porn industry. They would make me offers to come meet with them, but that was never something I could do, even being offered $80,000. I never liked being sexual and I think I would dissociate any time I had sex if I wasn't high. The company talked me into doing foot fetish videos. I didn't like it and thought it was weird and stupid, but the promise of a lot of money kept me going back. God would never allow me to see this money and I'm thankful because I'm certain I would have continued into worse things. During this time, I came across a business venture, which was selling prepaid porn cards. This was before smartphones and during a time when the internet was just beginning to be accessible by majority of the population. A prepaid porn card is a discrete way to access porn for an allotted amount of time without having to use your credit card number. This is before porn sites were free. This was especially prominent among married men looking to keep their indiscretions a secret.

One day as I was preparing to start this business, I drove from North Austin to South Austin. I passed many Nextel cellphone stores, but for some reason I was drawn to this particular store. I walked inside and there were two men and a woman at the counter. I was telling them what my plans were, and the woman began flashing me her breasts. I noticed a man in the back not saying much. He exited out the back of the store with a box of phones in his hands. He was an independent contractor that took phones to sell them outside of the store. I began talking about business cards and the man walked back in the store. One of the guys at the counter told me the guy that had just walked back in was on his way to get business cards and suggested I follow him. He agreed for me to follow him, so I left in my car and followed the quiet man that held the box in his hands. I had no idea what would happen next and how it would impact my life.

We arrived at the business card place. As I was standing with the quiet man, I began telling him all my plans of selling prepaid porn cards. As I was telling him my plans, he called me a church girl. He was in the store when the woman flashed her breasts at me so when he addressed me as "church girl," I was shocked.

I asked him, "Why do you call me that if you hear what I'm talking about?"

He responded, "Because your eyes are pure, you are a church girl."

I continued telling him how I never even went to church but he continued speaking of the purity of my eyes. We decided to go to Wendy's and get some food and I followed him in my car.

While we were ordering our food, he looked at my necklace and calmly said, "Your necklace is satanic."

I responded, "How?"

He replied again, "It's satanic."

I argued once more defending my necklace and telling him that it was a cross, and crosses couldn't be satanic. We got our food and went and sat in my car. As we were sitting there, he began telling me about my whole life. He told me Satan's plan for my life, which I was right on course for.

He said, "The person who gave you that, showed someone in their family because they were excited to buy it for you, but that person they showed cursed it."

The necklace came from Carlos. It was a gold rope chain and I always wanted one like it. He gave me the necklace after our daughter was born for a special occasion. At the time I owned it for about three years. The curse was to make me go crazy, go broke, and get fat and all those things happened to me before I repented of the sin in my life.

He went on to say, "The angels have been trying to get it off your neck, but you keep reattaching it."

When he said this, I knew he was telling the truth! I instantly remembered many times in Texas, Atlanta, and Sarasota when I would notice my necklace unclasped and the cross would not fall off it. It would dangle completely unclasped but seemed to be magnetized against my body and would never fall. It appeared to defy gravity and I would say, "Thank God!" and then clasp it back together. Another time I was taking off my necklace and the cross fell, and I heard it hit the terrazzo floor with a loud ding. I began searching for the cross, but I couldn't find it. I was planning to move in the next few weeks, so I told Ellis I would find it when we moved. I received a call from my dad later that week asking, "Are you missing a cross? I found it on your mother's pillow."

My mom lived about eight miles from my house and I know for a fact that cross fell off at my house.

The man continued talking to me and my mother called while he was talking. I told my mom what was happening, that I just met a man, and he was telling me about my life and the plan Satan had for my life. She was concerned, but I told her the peace I had when he would talk to me. I stayed there with the man for over six hours in the Wendy's parking lot. He was on the passenger side and people would continuously come up to his window. I saw him interact with homeless people and buy them food and lead them in prayer. I saw him tell a man from up north that his father's friend had cursed him to be wanderer, and that his mother was worried about him. He gave him money to call home from the payphone.

As I continued talking with the mysterious man, he began mentioning Satan's plan for my life in detail. He told me that Satan would lure me into the porn industry, and I would fall in love with a director and the director would give me AIDS. I began crying because I was literally waiting for a director to call me so we could meet up.

He said, "Why do you think he isn't calling?"

I replied, "I don't know."

He said, "Because I'm here talking to you."

I began telling him how when I was a little girl, I would hear the word AIDS and I would begin crying. I remember watching TV in the early nineties as the AIDS epidemic grew worse and they began making movies about HIV/AIDS. There was this one movie with Molly Ringwald I think, and I would watch it and cry. I didn't understand why I was crying exactly but AIDS was very terrifying for me to hear about. I even went to the clinic as a teen constantly for fear of having AIDS and not knowing it.

Before he left, he told me I had to get rid of the necklace. I always wanted this chain, and it was real gold, so I was skeptical. However, I knew all the things this man told me; nobody could've ever known. I asked him to throw it in the dumpster for me, but he said I had to be the one to do it. I told him how I had Fibromyalgia and didn't have the strength, but he insisted I had to throw it myself. I took the necklace off and placed it in the Wendy's bag with all my uneaten food. It was impossible to eat while hearing everything this man was telling me. All the food I didn't eat made the bag very heavy. I walked to the dumpster that was surrounded by a red brick wall that stood taller than the actual dumpster. As I threw the bag, I experienced an incredible force propel me. Right before my eyes, the bag fell out of sight beneath the brick into the dumpster. However, it ascended or almost defied gravity, levitated, and landed back on the brick ledge with the Wendy's logo facing me. The guy ran up to the top and knocked it into the dumpster.

We continued talking and he told me stories of witches and women who looked like regular people, but they really were not. I was reminded again of something that happened when I was in the therapeutic camp. Every day we ended the day around a campfire. I was sitting next to my friend who was Puerto Rican and Italian with deep brown hair and dark skin. We were sitting next to a bonfire on a bench with a group of other girls. We were laughing hard about something and as I opened my eyes she changed completely before my eyes. I leaned in for a split second to look closer and she remained in the form of an old wrinkled woman with white hair and a loud cackle. I was terrified and jumped off the bench into a ball and began screaming, demanding no one to come near me. I don't think I even used my feet to jump, it was unlike anything I had ever seen. Nobody else saw what I did, but the girl was mysteriously pulled from the program shortly after that night.

As we began to say our good-byes, I told him that I wanted to talk to him again very soon. I told him how peaceful it was to have him around and I hoped we could meet again. He told me, "Everyone says that but when I call, they won't answer." I vowed that when he called me, I would answer, I mean why wouldn't I answer? Well, when he did call me, I froze and no matter how bad I wanted to answer the phone, I couldn't. I was disappointed and couldn't understand why that happened. I often wondered the identity of that man and whether he was an angel sent from God…I am convinced he was! I never again met the director and quit foot fetish modeling forever!

Chapter X

*"Your ears shall hear a word behind you,
saying, "This is the way, walk in it," Whenever
you turn to the right hand Or whenever
you turn to the left."- Isaiah 30:21*

I started being Grammy's caretaker. After I dropped my daughter off at daycare, I would go to my mom's house to help Grammy shower and get dressed. I'd make food for her and take her to all her appointments. She was a big part of my daughter's life and my daughter would stay in Grammy's room, while playing babies with her. My daughter lived with me but spent most of the time either with my mom or my friend Ava because of my lifestyle.

I began dating someone else and selling more drugs. I struggled in college because I was always high and didn't want to go to class or I would miss money. My family tried to intervene sometimes by trying to ask me or figure out what was going on, but I don't think they understood, or they would have tried harder. I looked good on the outside and had a lot of material things, but I was sinking deeper and deeper on the inside. By this time, I cut ties with the lawyer because I let him down in Florida. I called him one more time with empty promises when Mike's lights got turned off. He sent me $700 and that was the last time I talked to him.

The guy I began dating began being abusive to me and terrorized me, but I couldn't get rid of him. When I tried, he showed up with a sawed-off shotgun and even told the neighbors if they hear a gunshot call the cops. He was messing everything up; my money, and my mind and I wanted him gone! I walked in my room one day and he was calling me his baby mama's name. He had been smoking wet (PCP), doing coke, and drinking bottles of liquor, and didn't even know who I was. He put his hands around my throat and began choking me. His friend walked in the room and got me free and then I left at once. I began praying for God to intervene. I stopped by another dope dealer's house and smoked a blunt when I received a phone call. He was outside hitting cars with a stick or something, looking for me. His friends begged me to come back. I told them I would not come back, even though it was my house. Eventually the police came and ran his name and took him to jail due to a warrant for violating parole. This was shocking because a few weeks prior he was pulled over while driving my car. I was in the backseat and there was a cookie (an ounce of cocaine that has been cooked into crack form) in the side of my front door that I had just bought. My front seat would not scoot up because of electrical issues and I could not get to the dope. Thank God my car wasn't searched and when the officer ran his name, his name was clear. However, on this night, a parole violation came back, and he was taken away. I knew God had heard my prayer and showed me mercy, but I didn't learn my lesson.

I continued selling dope and it was so obvious that even my neighbors reported me to my landlord. My landlord asked me if I was trafficking drugs and I acted dumb and made excuses for the traffic at my house. I had no financial need to sell drugs. My parents helped me, and I had government assistance, but like I said I was addicted to the street life. I continued helping the guy I was dating that got taken away that night with money for a lawyer and even went to see him in jail. I have no idea why, some part was excitement, but I think I was also scared that he would hurt me if I didn't help. When he was sentenced to prison and I knew he wouldn't be coming back I quit talking to him completely.

At this point, undercover officers would come to my door and try to get me to sell dope to them. I knew everyone in the area that did crack, and they were outsiders. I could tell by the language they were using and their uncomfortable demeanor as if they were trying to mimic the body language of a drug addict. I told them to never come to my door again and shut it. I began getting nervous and scared that my door would be kicked in soon. I decided to tell my mom what I had been doing and that I knew I was about to be taken to jail. I had a big screen TV and couches that I had been paying on bi-weekly. I didn't know I could give them back and receive no penalty if my payments were current, and I didn't want to mess up my credit. I decided to ask my mom for help. My mom and I went to the furniture store and it cost $800.00 to own both couches and the big screen TV. My mom made a $400.00 payment, but as the cashier deducted the $400.00 the price jumped up higher. This continued for several minutes. I then heard a voice clear as day speak, "These aren't yours anyway, give them up and I will move you from here." I immediately told my mom that I didn't want them and never mind. My mom looked at me confused and I told her they weren't mine anyway. She agreed and we left the store. I don't think I understood what was happening or who I was hearing, but I believed the voice I heard. Just as the voice promised, He moved me several counties over to start a new life, just me and my daughter, and my friend Ava took over as caretaker for Grammy.

Chapter XI

"For what will it profit a man if he gains the whole world, and loses his own soul?" – Mark 8:36

I began living in a suburb in Austin and was finally out of the small town. I was excited for a new beginning but kept up with my old ways. I did vow to not sell drugs and I kept that promise for a while. I was still around people who would sell drugs and I was still getting high on weed and coke and drinking sometimes. I enjoyed having excessive amounts of money, so I dated dope dealers.

Just a few months after moving there I began dating a guy named Lucas, who was a few months younger than me. He had just been released from prison and was involved in many aspects of the street life. I stopped doing cocaine. Many times, throughout my life I would be clean during relationships, because that was the ultimate drug for me. However, even that began to not be enough, especially if I was left alone. There was a fight in my soul. I was constantly conflicted between what was familiar and what God would show me. I remember asking Lucas, "Do you think it's possible to get what you see in your mind... like in real life?"

I would later learn these were visions God was giving me for my future.

I had no idea how to act once I heard God's voice in that furniture store a year earlier and often thought I was losing my mind. Lucas and I began going to church with my daughter sometimes and I would begin having a deep desire to find God. I was still focused on getting the prepaid porn cards and we went to church with someone I planned to incorporate into a related business. We named the business Twisted Entertainment which consisted of producing music for up and coming rappers, much of which was funded through the prepaid porn cards. I thought if I gave money to good causes, like stopping childhood sexual abuse, then this business would be legitimate in God's eyes. I was utterly deceived!

Lucas and I had been hanging out for a few months, but it was a typical hood-type relationship. I was never really his girlfriend, even though I thought I was. I talked him into buying me those prepaid porn cards I wanted, so I could start my own business. My goal was to be a millionaire before I graduated college. I had such grandiose thinking and would often go into manic episodes, which led me to think I could achieve the impossible without God! He rejected me a lot and it seemed to make me want him more. I couldn't stand being alone, but I also hated being at his family's house so I would choose to stay at my house. I was very jealous of the relationship he had with his family because they were very close, and that closeness was what I wanted and was missing. I'd get very triggered and would rather stay at home alone than be around them.

About the time I broke up with him I found out I was pregnant with my son. There were times I wouldn't see Lucas for a month. I thought if I wasn't so clingy, he would want me, but he didn't. Lucas could be very cruel to me especially when he was around his friends. He constantly tried to embarrass me or act like I was slow and would disrespect me. However, I treated him bad too! I would encourage him, then tear him down. One minute I would build him up and tell him to go to college since he already had his GED. I would help him get his paperwork done but then go into a rage and tear all his stuff up.

We decided to stay together for our son, and it was torturous for both of us. I was miserable with or without him and looking back I was not pleasant to be around at all. During this time, my mom would encourage me to go to church. I didn't really want to go but I would take my daughter to the same church her daycare was located. I felt so out of place with all these married couples. I was noticeably pregnant with my son and in addition I already had my daughter, but I was alone with no dad for them. I felt everyone staring and not many were very friendly towards me, but I continued going anyways.

Chapter XII

*"Do not be deceived, God is not mocked;
for whatever a man sows, that he
will also reap."- Galatians 6:7*

By the time I was twenty-one, I was about eight and a half months pregnant. My family was visiting for Christmas and my mom suggested I stay at her friend's house that was out of town. I was staying at my mom's friend's house alone. I honestly did not see staying with my mom's friend as bad, but after telling people, they pointed out how messed up it was that I was the only one not staying at my mom's house. I agreed it was messed up because I wasn't on drugs during this time, but I would have rageful outbursts, so maybe that's why she chose not to have me there. I was very emotionally unstable and seemed to be mostly triggered around my family.

I felt like I was going into labor and I called Lucas and his homeboy answered. Anytime someone had his phone it was because he was with me, so I knew he was with someone else and was cheating on me. I drove myself to the nearby hospital and they took me by ambulance to Austin, where I was due to give birth. It ended up being false labor and I had to call my neighbor to come get me, since my car was forty-five miles away in another hospital parking lot. I was so embarrassed about being cheated on and did not want to tell my family. My mom was calling me wondering where I was and thought I ran off to use drugs, but I still wouldn't tell her. My aunt happened to be coming through my neighborhood and was headed to my mom's and I caught a ride back with her. I was still embarrassed, but I finally told my mom what happened. I had never been cheated on to my knowledge, so this was a huge blow to my ego.

During this time, I was distraught and full of anxiety. I remembered Mike's girlfriend was prescribed Vicodin when she was pregnant for a car wreck injury. Despite never taking pills I decided to try them since his girlfriend was proof it was okay to take pills while pregnant. I took a pill, and I broke it in half. I had never taken pills other than mental health medicine. I ate a few crackers to help me not throw up. What I discovered was that pills would numb all my emotions and that began years of a pill addiction. I don't think I was physically addicted to the pills, but I was absolutely addicted to them numbing my emotions.

I wish I could say I never got high during my pregnancy with my son, but I did on a few occasions. To the glory of God my son was born healthy and excels academically, athletically and has no signs of the life I lived, and God has healed him of asthma. I hate I didn't give the same start to my son that my daughter received. I hate how selfish and inconsiderate I was even towards my own children. I want to encourage anyone reading this that it is possible for God to remove the guilt of even these things. God promises, "If we confess our sins, He is faithful and just to forgive us our sins and to cleanse us from all unrighteousness" (1 John 1:9). Not only does God promise to forgive us but He also promises to cleanse us. The blood of Jesus was shed to not only redeem your soul, but also to cleanse your conscience. While I may cry as I write this, I am no longer held in the chains of guilt and shame that paralyzed me from moving forward or kept me running to get high. He broke the chains. Although I can experience the emotions as I re-tell my past, it no longer grips me into destruction.

I think part of the reason I struggled with addiction so much after moving out of my parent's house was that running away no longer provided the escape I needed. I had my own house and growing up I was running from the pain by leaving my family's house. Now I was alone and in worse pain than ever. I could no longer run, so I had to either face it or numb it. I chose to numb it.

Chapter XIII

*"To everything there is a season,
A time for every purpose under heaven:
A time to be born, And a time to die;
A time to plant, And a time to pluck
what is planted"- Ecclesiastes 3:1-2*

One day Grammy fell while she was holding her chest. I still remember that day like it was yesterday. We called the ambulance, and they took her forty-five miles to Austin to the same hospital I was due to have my son at the following month. I would go up there and visit with her but always expected she would come home. One day they wheeled her off for a procedure and the next thing I knew she was in ICU on life-support. For the next couple of weeks, I would visit her at the hospital and try to prepare for her death mentally. Nothing could prepare me for what happened.

On February 16, 2007, I gave birth to my precious son, Isaiah Orlando. I spent early labor in ICU at my grandmother's side. As much as it hurt to have my son while my grandma was in ICU, I was thankful I could be with her and that my mom did not have to go in between hospitals. There are so many hospitals in Austin and for God to take her to that one, over a month earlier showed me that He's in control and that He loves us.

I called Lucas after he was born, and he came up there to see our son for a little bit. My little brother Maxx stayed the night with me that night and the next day Lucas came back. I made Lucas walk up to ICU to see my grandma, because he thought I was lying, and he sat there as I cried over my grandma. Lucas stayed with me that night and the next day my grandma was taken off life support. I chose not to go in the room but stayed in my room praying and crying. I was taking full advantage of the pain pills they give you after birth in hopes of numbing the pain of my grandma's death.

The day my grandma died was also the day I had to name my son and sign the birth certificate. I did not want him to have Lucas' last name, so I signed it in the bathroom behind his back. I also didn't trust Lucas was going to stay around and didn't want a different name than my kids. The entire time I was pregnant, I planned to name my son Isaiah Orlando. At this point I didn't even know Isaiah was in the Bible; I heard it from the Halle Berry movie when I was ten years old. At the last moment I got very confused as to which name to put first. I like the idea of his initials spelling OIL, so I switched it to Orlando Isaiah. As we left the hospital, I went to call Grammy to tell her I had my baby only to realize she died. We left the hospital and went to show Lucas' family our new baby. It was surreal and he held my hand and I thought this may last, but within a few days I knew he would be gone and as sad as it made me, I never felt good around him anyway.

I ended up going to the vital statistic office and amending the name of my son to the original name I chose, Isaiah Orlando. I was due to be back in college when he was five weeks old, but there was a problem. I was not able to add him to the waiting list for childcare until two weeks after his birth, which made it impossible for me to return to college on time. I walked out to my mailbox and opened a letter from the daycare assistance agency. In the envelope was a letter dated two weeks before my son's birth with the amended name, Isaiah Orlando. I hadn't even had the new birth certificate yet and the fact it predated his birth by several weeks led me to thank God again for another miracle!

Chapter XIV

"No one can come to Me unless the Father who sent Me draws him; and I will raise him up at the last day." – John 6:44

When my son was fifteen days old, I showed up to a Bible study at a local church near my apartment. It was my daughter, my son, and me. I walked in there carrying the weight of a boulder of pain, hurt, rejection, and depression. I was invited to this church by a lady who was my son's daycare teacher. She used to go to the church I went to when I was pregnant with him. I felt so much love as I walked into this small church. It had only been open for a year and although I decided to start by only attending Wednesdays, I continued going back week after week.

I had not changed my ways yet, but God was dealing with my heart. I would often be on the block smoking weed and let everyone know I would be back in a little bit. When they asked where I was going, I'd reply, "I'm going to Bible study." They eagerly asked if they could go too! It was not uncommon for me to bring dope dealers into the church and they welcomed them with open arms. The Pastor's name was Pastor Jones and he had a wife, Mrs. Jones. She took me under her wing and began to spend nearly every day with me. I'd go grocery shopping, to the pharmacy, to her house, even eat at nice restaurants. She and Pastor Jones would lavish love on me and my children. She would often talk to me on my cell phone for six hours each day. This was before unlimited minutes, so my mom wanted to know who on earth I was talking to that much. When I told her the Pastor's wife, Mrs. Jones, she paid a lot of money to get me unlimited minutes. Mrs. Jones later told me that she felt if she could keep me talking then she could keep me alive.

I decided to get baptized. A few days before I was baptized, I ran into my old best-friend, Briana. I saw her outside of her grandma's apartment as I was driving by and I stopped by. We hugged and immediately she looked at me and said, "Michelle you look different!" She went on to comment how I no longer had a tan from tanning beds and my nails were no longer done. She continued looking me up and down and commented that one thing that didn't change was that I still had my toes done. We laughed and I began telling her about Jesus. I told her that I no longer felt the need to have those material things. My face shined with the glory of God and there's no doubt I had truly received Jesus Christ, even though I hadn't truly surrendered it all! I invited Briana to church and let her know I would be getting baptized if she wanted to come. She eagerly accepted, and also wanted to be baptized. We then began spending our days together.

The night before we were to be baptized, we stopped at a gas station and a man came up and offered us cocaine. I knew it was the devil. We told him no but had him take our picture together. I still have that picture and it reminds me how much God had healed me in that brief time, but also how imperative it is to read the Bible regularly and apply what you read. In James 1:22 it says, "But be doers of the word, and not hearers only, deceiving yourselves." I was baptized in May of 2007 along with Briana and my little brother, Maxx. My mom and dad came, and my big brother, Mike. On this day, my children were dedicated to God. My daughter, Aja, was four years old and my son, Isaiah, was three months old and I had just turned twenty-two years old. My dad even wanted to get baptized, but since he was raised Catholic, he didn't. I still believe God will grant him another opportunity to repent and be baptized in the name of Jesus!

I began spending more time at church including choir practice on Saturday, church service on Sunday, midweek Bible study, and women's Bible study. I loved being there, and on many occasions, I would meet Mrs. Jones at the church, and she would pray over me. This was a very small church, and we had a teen ministry that I was put in charge of. I would go over pre-made lessons with them. This was an incentive to keep me there because I didn't want to let the teens down, but I was also a baby Christian and had no business being in leadership. I believe Mrs. Jones did the best she knew how with me, and her intentions were pure and completely out of love. I would only read enough of the Bible to go over the lesson, but I didn't actually spend time reading the Bible for myself, which kept me in the same street mentality. I didn't know the magnitude of the sins I was continuously committing. During the time I would teach the teens, Pastor Jones would give the sermon, so I often missed it. Even with the Bible studies I was not growing at the rate I would have liked to because I didn't study or read outside of church.

My family and Briana would continue coming sometimes to my church, which was forty minutes away from where they lived. I appreciated they would come visit and watch me sing, even though I wasn't very good. I always wanted to sing, and I began learning to sing beautiful songs to God. I had the opportunity to be trained by a renowned vocal coach.

There were some radical changes although not as radical as I may have wanted. I remember having a lot of stolen make-up and I called Mrs. Jones and asked if I should go to the store to return it. She advised me the store would not forgive me like God and I would go to jail, so just stop stealing moving forward. I also began to be convicted of the prepaid porn cards that were under my bed. I called Mrs. Jones and told her I needed to burn them. They were estimated to be worth $8,500, but I couldn't stand the feeling of having them. I was excited to dispose of them. She invited me to her house to burn the cards. I showed up with a large Tupperware container filled to the top with stacks of cards. At first Pastor Jones said, "You can't burn that here!" He thought it was filled with marijuana. Mrs. Jones went on to tell him what it really was, and we went and put them in the Bar-B-Q pit, saturated them in lighter fluid, and lit a match. I stood there watching them burn in amazement of where God had brought me.

The Holy Spirit began pointing out the way I treated people and the narcissistic tendencies I used in my daily life. I would cry, repent, and try hard to change. During this time, I began feeling evil follow me and often would feel as though I was being watched. I would have sleep paralysis dreams and feel spiders crawling out of my head and skin as I slept. I was constantly waking up thinking I had spiders everywhere and could not understand why I was hallucinating if I wasn't on hard drugs. I didn't know Satan comes after you with the hounds of hell when you come to Jesus, so I just continued sticking close to Mrs. Jones.

About this time, I was being tormented with Fibromyalgia and decided to go to the doctor. I was put on muscle relaxers, narcotic pain pills, and medicine for anxiety and PTSD, along with the mood stabilizers for bipolar and anti-depressants. This was an opportune time for the devil to weigh me down because I was a baby Christian and terrified of being completely sober because of the flashbacks of being raped. They were extremely intrusive thoughts and caused me to dissociate and make me feel like I was outside of my body. I began to abuse the pills at unprecedented levels. Mrs. Jones was worried about me because I took more anti-depressants than her sister who had terminal cancer. She tried to get me to see I had a problem, but I was in denial.

Chapter XV

"Be sober, be vigilant; because your adversary the devil walks about like a roaring lion, seeking whom he may devour."- 1 Peter 5:8

Two months after I was baptized, Lucas said to come get some money for our son. Messed up on pills, and still emotionally wounded by him cheating, I got to where he said to meet. He wasn't there when I got there but his sister and some other girls were. I saw these girls coming out and I got mentally ready to defend myself, which didn't make sense since his sister and I was really close. When I got out the car, I started swinging. They were overpowering me, so I went in my backseat to get the hammer that I was using for the bulletin board at church. They later told me I was tripping, and it wasn't like that. However, police got involved, and I caught my first charge as an adult for aggravated assault with a deadly weapon.

By the grace of God, I was never indicted, but I gave no glory or thanks to God. I was very prideful and took all the credit for the miraculous outcome of that case. I continued fighting and getting arrested. I never spent more than twelve days in jail. Mrs. Jones told me, "Michelle, if you ever go to prison it won't be for drugs, but it will be for your anger!" I was shocked at what she said and began to agree I had a problem, although I don't think I ever admitted it. I continued to be in church regularly and was great at evangelizing the hood by just telling someone I was on my way to church or bringing up God in conversations He usually wouldn't be brought up in. I shared the same testimony I shared with Briana about joy and the changes God made in my life. I was excited but was still living in disobedience. Reading the Bible for yourself is crucial and I often wonder what would have happened if I would have made it a priority.

I would have periods of time where I would do well, but every time I went to visit my family, I would stop to get cocaine and stronger pills on the way there. It was one thing to be sober at my house, but it was impossible to be sober at my parents. This is because I was stuck at the age I was when I was abused by the family friend. So even though everything after was worse, it never affected me the same. There was another family holiday where my mom offered to get me a hotel room so I could be comfortable, given all the family that was in from out of town. Looking back, I know she did it to try to keep me from causing problems, but it just made me feel rejected. I was happy that I didn't have to endure staying around the family and I was not punished for not being there. I had a license to stay gone.

Mike stopped by because he was struggling with overcoming a meth addiction and when I answered the door, he confided in me that he was having a hard time. I told him not to do meth and instead went and got the plate that had an ounce of coke on it and offered it to him. In my mind coke wasn't as bad as meth. He got high with me, but then realized I would probably die by using that much so he finally told my parents. There was an attempted intervention after it was discovered I was at a hotel by myself and had an ounce of cocaine. I had a lot of Xanax, coke, and an entire bottle of Sangria and was taking it all together. I went to sit down on my bed to put on my clothes and passed out until later that night. When I woke up it was dark, and I decided it was better to be late than not come at all. I completely missed Thanksgiving dinner that night. That's when I was met with family asking me where the rest of the coke was, which I lied and said it was gone. It seems as if after I came to Christ, I got much worse on every level. That's what addiction does, it effects every area of your life negatively and keeps you from walking in the newness of life Christ died to give you. Oh, how I wish I would've read His word and obeyed it!

One day I visited a church member to give her food and milk. I had never met her, but I was excited to do something for someone else. Looking back, I see Satan was setting up a trap for me. I began hanging out with her to avoid being alone. She was in her forties and had two sons that were in middle school and my daughter's age. One day I asked if she wanted to ride to Austin so I could run an errand. She agreed and on the way home, she asked me to stop at some apartments. I began to feel something wasn't right and later found out that she bought crack. I was sad inside and didn't want any part of this and I felt bad for her. I had never done crack before. Coke and crack were two completely different calibers. To me and the people I grew up around, the worst thing that could happen was to become a crack head. They were disrespected and a joke to everyone and people treated crack addicts horribly. However, cocaine was a totally different thing. The people who had coke were usually wealthy. Coke was for average people. Crack was for fiends. She asked if she could smoke it at my house, and since my kids were at daycare, I allowed it. She would continue asking me if I wanted any but for months, I would say no, and continue taking my pills. I would help her get crack from people in the suburbs, so she didn't have to drive to the hood in Austin.

Eventually I gave in and began smoking crack with her and for nearly a year I could not get high. Then one day I was addicted. I began to get so deep in addiction, and nobody knew. I began going back to dope dealers and buying wholesale as though I were going to sell it, but I would smoke it all. I couldn't believe I had turned into a dope fiend. We reap what we sow, and I had sold so much crack to other people and destroyed their lives and now I was reaping the same thing I sowed into their lives. My pride kept me from getting help. I couldn't utter the words crack. I would tell my mom years later that I was addicted to cocaine, but never said crack! It was yet another blow to my pride and I couldn't believe I was a dope fiend!

I began hanging out with this dope dealer who was only nineteen and I was twenty-three. We usually just chilled but one day I had sex with him while we were on ecstasy and we continued in a relationship after that. I was horrible to him and violently assaulted him many times. I would break his glasses and take his dope and then call the cops on him so he would have to leave. I knew he didn't have dope on him because I took it so I knew he wouldn't go to jail, but it was still so wrong. We would get back together and takes turns bonding each other out of jail. This whole time he had no idea I was smoking crack. I didn't always get high when I was with him, but I began getting more desperate. I was filled with darkness and the addiction to crack took over my life. We eventually broke up and he went to jail for a while.

Chapter XVI

"But it shall come to pass, if you do not obey the voice of the Lord your God, to observe carefully all His commandments and His statutes which I command you today, that all these curses will come upon you and overtake you."- Deuteronomy 28:15

All throughout this I remained in college and from the outside I looked okay unless you looked into my eyes. I have no idea how my children were never taken from me. Honestly, I should have given them to my mom, but I never wanted anyone to know what I was really doing. During the times I would be single I would begin writing an ex named Kris from Florida. He was sentenced to ten years when I was sent to the therapeutic camp. We always wrote each other every few years but the relationship was insignificant. I began planning to pick him up when he would be released.

I decided to move closer to Austin and further from my church. I was barely hanging on but continued living a double life, teaching the teens one minute and doing drugs the next. One day I was on a dating site and met someone from my hometown in Florida. We would just talk online or on the phone from time to time, but I had no idea that I had met this man a decade earlier. One day he calls me from a Miami area code, which was not the area code I was expecting. I asked, "Who is this?" and he replied with his name. In an instant I had a flashback of the day I was looking at Sarasota's Most Wanted with Carlos sitting next to me. This was the man who raped and sodomized me and forced me to walk around the hood as his girlfriend. He told me his real name… the same name on the wanted poster. I could hear Mrs. Jones' voice in my head saying, "If you want mercy you need to show mercy and forgive!"

So, I said, "Do you go by Cash?"

He said, "Yes."

I said, "Do you remember me?"

He said, "What do you mean?"

I said, "Go look at my picture and tell me who I am!"

I began telling him about him raping me at that house and on the school bus and everything he did to me. He insisted it was consensual, but I wouldn't stand for it! I began telling him that even though he meant to destroy me that I was okay, and I struggled for a while, but I was okay! Looking back, I was not okay at all, but I wanted to feel strong and not let him think he won! I told him to admit what he did and apologize to me and he finally did!

I told him, "I forgive you, but I never want to talk to you again!" That was the last time I spoke to him. I later learned this man had been arrested for multiple rapes to both adolescents and senior citizens (some of which were at gunpoint), kidnapping, and attempted murder, yet somehow, he remained free. Learning this helped relieve the guilt I had been carrying for responding the way I did when he raped me by pretending to be his girlfriend. Looking back, I can see how forgiving him was leading up to the family friend I desperately needed to forgive yet was the hardest to forgive; even though I wanted to forgive him more than anyone!

A few months after moving to my new apartment, it was time for Kris to be released and I decided to go pick him up in Florida. My mother wrote me a heartfelt letter warning me against my decision and mailed it to my house and I still refused to listen. I would later see everything she wrote in her warning come to pass. I went against all advice and counsel and was determined to keep my word to him. I took pride in my loyalty to him, although I was completely disloyal to those who should've mattered, like my children and family. I should have been loyal to God and I wish I had, but regardless of whether I went or not, I was already being unfaithful to Him.

Everything that could have gone wrong the day I left for Florida, did. I missed my flight and once I got on another flight, the suitcases fell on top of my head as I tried to put them in the storage compartments. I knew I was drastically moving out of God's will for my life, but I stayed focused on the fairytale I created in my head.

I was messed up on pills the whole flight, and during layovers in Atlanta I stayed at the bar, drinking with strangers. By the time I arrived in Florida and got the rental car, I was hours late picking him up from prison. I had no concept of time and was out of my mind. Before I went to pick him up, I ended up at a house party with strangers, I still can't remember where I met them, and it's a miracle I didn't end up robbed or killed. I was so drunk and high on pills I couldn't read or follow the directions on my phone. I asked someone from the party if they could drive to the prison and let me follow in my rental so that I would not get lost. They agreed.

I remember walking up to the prison gate and told them who I was there to pick up. Within a few minutes Kris came walking out. He handed me the $100 they give to people who are being released. However, within a short time Kris took control of all my money, which was at least $1,000, both in my bank account and in cash. I was quite easy to control because I was always intoxicated. He drove all the way to Sarasota, which was about six hours away. I was passed out the entire time he drove. I was so foolish and reckless.

We arrived at a friend's house and stayed there, and I began doing more pills and nodding off while talking to her. She was in recovery from addiction. I would tell her about Jesus and even led her in the "Sinner's Prayer." I had no idea that repentance was part of receiving Jesus Christ. Again, not reading the Bible myself really did a disservice to me and those I was around. My dear friend would die a few years later from a drug overdose and it wasn't until recently that I realized how I mislead her so greatly. I had no business talking about Jesus while I was high and drunk. I wish I could have another opportunity to lead her to Christ the right way, but it is too late!

Kris would control where I could go and who I could see. He would make me wait in the car while he went into some places. I didn't know it then but later realized he was inside smoking crack. I didn't know the same addiction I was currently in bondage to, he had ten years ago when we first met, and immediately upon release from prison, went right back to!

We spent two weeks in Florida and right before we left, I canceled Kris's plane ticket back to Texas. I had second thoughts and didn't want him to come back with me. He got angry and when I tried to fix it, the airline told me there was no way to undo the damage. At this time, I realized the money was gone, which I couldn't figure out how, but later realized he had been spending it on crack. We went to Tampa and I took him to the bus station before I missed my flight back to Texas. I told him I would get him a bus ticket somehow. I ended up calling Mrs. Jones and she reluctantly bought him a ticket. He was angry that she wouldn't buy a plane ticket and he had to ride the bus. I wish I wouldn't have cared about pleasing others and left him in Sarasota and cut my losses then.

From the time of Kris's arrival, we fought. He was always drunk and would disappear for days at a time. This was still before I knew he was smoking crack. I was so naïve to think he would end up downtown around the homeless, because it was hard for him to adjust to life after doing ten years. He was originally supposed to go into a halfway house, which I had already orchestrated, and this was to help me safeguard the Section 8 Housing I had while finishing my last two years of college. Kris never went into the half-way house and within a short time my family decided to try to give him a chance, so that they could see me. To my surprise my family loved him, and we continued going to my church. He began staying at my parents' house during the week while working for my dad and I remained in my apartment going to school. He was very helpful to my mom, helping her clean and cook. He was a real con-artist and at the very least a textbook sociopath.

I continued juggling college, kids, church, and crack addiction. I began going to church less and stopped teaching the teens. Kris began staying at my house more often and figured out I was smoking crack. I was ashamed so I wouldn't smoke in front of him, and he always said he didn't want any...until the day he did! We began smoking a lot of dope because I could get it so cheap and none of my homies knew I was smoking crack. We fought a lot, and police would get called, but he never went to jail... I did. He whispered to me one day, "They will never take me to jail. I've lived with them for ten years and we are like family!" I began to see his con- man ways even more but didn't make him leave. One instance, he was trying to take my car and, in an attempt to stop him, I got on the hood and told him no. He pulled off and started driving crazy through the apartment complex, hitting sharp turns. When he finally stopped, he said, "Do you know why you didn't die?"

I said, "Because of God!"

He replied, "No, because I chose to let you live!"

I eventually got kicked out of my apartment and off Section 8 and was forced to move back to my parents for the first time since moving out in high school. Kris and I would often leave the kids with my mom, go to Austin, smoke crack, and then come back home like nothing happened. I did not get along with my family and he often would make me paranoid about my family and try to turn them against me. I didn't know who to trust and it was getting to be too much! Mike was living there too, and I didn't get along with him at all. I chose to leave my kids there and move into my SUV and slept in my college parking lot. I did this for at least a month and stayed clean and sober the whole time! My grades got better because it was cold, and I had no choice but to be in the library. I would get hotel rooms from local churches on the weekends so I could see my kids. I eventually got a one bedroom near my church and wanted to stay clean but started back smoking crack and allowed Kris to move in. My kids remained with my mom and I would go there on the weekend or my kids would come to my apartment. My electricity was cut off once when they were there, and Kris would go turn it on illegally. I was getting tired of this life and soon decided to leave him and move back home with my mom and kids.

Chapter XVII

"Pride goes before destruction, And a haughty spirit before a fall." – Proverbs 16:18

I struggled hard at my mom's house. I continued driving to Austin for class, but had a tough time staying in class and usually ended up getting high on crack. I can remember falling asleep with a crack pipe in my hand and tons of dope all over the floor. I had so much dope it was ridiculous, and it was a miracle I lived through it! I was so depressed and could not believe I lost everything and had to be back with the family I ran away from as a teen. I never took responsibility for any of the decisions I made but blamed everyone else around me. I remember Mrs. Jones telling me years earlier, "You have the favor of God and you don't want to lose that. Once you lose it, it's very hard to get it back!" I laughed and thought I was untouchable, yet here I was clearly no longer in God's favor! I was so angry that I lost it all and blamed everything on Kris, never looking at my clear rebellion against God! I was stuck with no help and he just let me lose it and never tried to help me. I wasn't used to being with a man like that! I couldn't see it then, but all these events were breaking me to the point where I would soon truly surrender my will!

I remember one day laying in Maxx's bed, since I had no room at my mom's house, and I said aloud, "Well, I will either stay asleep or stay high until I leave my mom's house!" That is exactly what I did too! I was still in heavy drug addiction and it grew even worse! The people I used to hustle with six years prior gave me wholesale prices because nobody had any idea I was using. They say it is the free stuff or cheap stuff that will kill you and I would have to agree!

When my money would run out or I was waiting for my scripts to be refilled, I began setting people up to jack them. I usually was alone when I did this and did it on foot. I remember going to the places I set as the designated spot and running through the plan alone, hours before they arrived. I was very calculated and it's scary how successful I was at strategizing. The thought that went into this was definitely a skill that I was using in the wrong way. I knew how to pick the victim and lure him away and would do it all myself and escape with their money. At one point I brought in this guy Dayton to help and I would lure the victim to the hood under the guise that if they bought me some dope, they could sleep with me. I would take off with their money and get in Dayton's car that was waiting for me on the other side of the fence.

Honestly, I got a high from doing this and began doing it way too often even according to Dayton. Dayton told me I needed to stop because I was going to get killed. I knew he was right and honestly took it as a warning from God. I totally stopped setting people up, but not before one of the victims found out who I was and began calling my mother's school where she taught telling her what I had done! I was terrified for my family and kids, and I kept praying to God to cover my family even though I had done this awful thing! I would not accept responsibility when my mom confronted me, and I blamed it on the victim knowing I was wrong. I was trying to harden my heart to keep from feeling bad for the victim.

After this, I still would meet people and have them buy a quarter ounce of dope and would stay with them until it was gone. One night I met up with Dayton and I brought a guy to buy dope. I left with that guy and later, I believe I had a heart attack. I had been smoking a lot back to back. I hit it again and fell to my knees. I couldn't talk and my heart was beating so fast. My chest hurt and I felt all this pressure like my heart was about to explode. This other guy who was there too looked at me and talked calmly and touched my forehead and kept saying, "Stay with us...it's okay...stay with us." I focused on him touching my forehead, thinking, "Michelle, you can't die here! They will either leave you in this building alone or get charged for your death!" Amazing what we can think about at a time like that. I managed after a few minutes to get up, and honestly it was more out of duty for them not to get in trouble.

I continued smoking the rest of the day. The dope I got was so pure it often had to be cooked a second time. If it wasn't, it was not smokable and would combust into flames. Only Satan would give me something so good and strong, reeling me further into addiction. I preferred not to have to use sex to get drugs. For so long I had money or pills to sell or trade but once those pills were gone and the addiction had taken hold, I would close my eyes while doing unspeakable things for dope. I could not believe I had turned into this person. I would never out right sell my body and for a while it made me feel better that both people were involved to the same degree. Now I accept that what I did is the equivalent of prostitution. It's hard to even admit, but it's the truth and the truth sets us free, so I must share it!

Chapter XVIII

"The strong spirit of a man sustains him in bodily pain or trouble, but a weak and broken spirit who can raise up or bear?" – Proverbs 18:14 (AMPC)

During this time, I began leaving my kids with my mom for extended periods of time so I could go to Austin and get high. One day I got some weak dope and decided to try one more time before going back home. I had a substantial bit of money that I left at home so I wouldn't spend too much or stay gone too long. I decided to stop at a gas station in a known drug area. I got out of my car like I was pumping gas and signaled one of the guys to come over. I began telling him I needed a pack because I just got robbed. Using the term pack signified that I didn't smoke dope and I knew that was important to say. He looked over his shoulder and then the higher up guy came over and I repeated what I just told his associate. I told them I was from Marble Falls and was taking it back there. This was intentional so that they'd know selling to me wouldn't take from them making money. I told them if the people liked it, I'd be back to get more. They didn't know I smoked, and I was always able to speak and talk like I was one of them.

My brother Mike was always amazed at how men in the street would listen to me. I didn't look like a dope fiend and had been around dope dealers since I was in middle school. I knew what to say, how to act, and how to stand. These became my mannerisms and even when I wanted to turn it off and present a different person, I couldn't for very long before it would show again. So, the head guy told me to meet him down the street. He gave it to me along with his number and told me to call him JT. This began a relationship of business and at times I messed around with him, but it was mostly just business. I gained his trust, and he would take me to his mom's house out in the suburbs. This whole time he still didn't know I smoked. He loved taking bars (Xanax), and I got ninety of them prescribed to me every month, so he would often buy from me too. He began taking me to the spot he got his dope and I had been there before with a couple of different people. This made him trust me more.

One day JT and his brother were at a hotel and I went there to meet up with them. I got my own room there and had been in there getting high. I had a bad feeling, so I decided to go through all my Rx bottles, and I found one crack rock in it. I made sure I didn't have anything else on me except my pipe and I walked out of the room to meet them in the parking lot. They were getting aggravated because JT's brother had a trespassing warrant there and he didn't want the office to see him and call the law. We began walking to my car and I realized I locked my keys in the car. I tried to go back to my room to let them chill there, but my room card wasn't working because it had been demagnetized. JT went with me to the office to get a new card. At that moment two police cars pulled up. As I was standing in the lobby in front of customers and in front of a large pane window, directly in front of the police officers, JT threw an ounce of crack to me and by reflex, I caught it. I did not have time to think so I unzipped my pants and fit as much as I could in my private area. It hurt so bad, but it was my only chance to not get caught with dope in my hand. I was surprised none of the guests saw me or said anything if they did. I was not able to walk or sit right but I tried my best to not let the discomfort show.

    They called us outside and began asking what we were doing there, and they ran our names. JT had a warrant and was put in the back of the police car. The hotel manager came out yelling at JT's brother that they told him not to come back, so that is when I knew that it was the hotel that called the police. JT's brother left and then came back to pick up his car that was on the property and the manager saw him and had him arrested. The police ran my name, and I was shocked when it came back that I had a warrant for a bad check. I had never had my name come back on a warrant check before. I had a crack pipe in my wallet and feared that what I had been hiding in the dark was about to come to light in front of JT and his brother, and I was so embarrassed! The manager came out apologizing to me and refunded my money as I sat on the curb in handcuffs. I was so nervous about going to jail with an ounce of crack. Taking drugs into a correctional facility was a huge risk, but I had to take it or have a 100% chance of going to prison. I'm not sure if JT or his brother ever saw the crack pipe.

    When I got to booking, I kept asking the officers if this would be on my record and how I was going to graduate from college that year. They told me in Austin it would show as a traffic citation and not on a criminal background check. That brought some relief, but I was so angry. The intake area of the jail was arranged like a lobby of a bus station with men on one side and women on the other. You could get up and go to the bathroom whenever you wanted, so I decided I needed to go to the bathroom and flush the dope. I got up and flushed it for fear that I would be checked once I was sent to the back to sleep. I had always been bonded out right away, so this whole event was different than the times before. I began thinking about Kris and knew he must have stolen my checks because I did not write bad checks. I began praying that wherever he was, that he would be arrested. Many hours past and I was finally called to the women's housing area to await my first appearance with the magistrate in the morning.

In the morning as I walked into the area where the magistrate judge read the charges and set the bond, I saw none other than Kris being booked. I began yelling at him from across the jail that it was his fault I was in there. He began laughing and smiling which made me even angrier! At the same time, I acknowledged God seemed to have heard my prayer. The guard warned me to get in line and be quiet, so I did but I was fuming with Kris. He was never bothered being locked up. He spent the majority of his life in prison and it was just like home to him.

I continued to walk into the magistrate office and saw JT and his brother. They asked what I did with it and I told them I flushed it. They both had lawyers on retainer and got out that day. The judge read out my charge including the charge of drug paraphernalia, which I was sure that JT knew what that meant, although it could have been many things.

I was still so scared for anyone to know the truth about the crack addiction! Any other addiction was fine, but not that one! I heard my charge, and I received a PR (Personal Recognizance) bond, which meant if I said I would show up for court and sign a paper, I was free. However, they made an added condition and that was my parents had to sign for me. My parents refused because I guess Kris had called them from jail and they thought we were together, and they were then against me being around him. They didn't believe that the two of us could be arrested an hour from where we both lived, and both end up in the Travis County jail on the same night and not have been arrested together. I guess I shouldn't have prayed for him to get arrested after all.

Since my parents wouldn't sign, I had to wait for Williamson County to come pick me up, which took twelve days. Williamson County finally came, and I was in jail a few hours before being released with time served due to the stay in Travis County. The charge was behind a $20.00 check that bounced, and I knew I was not the one who wrote it. I always wrote checks for a specific amount if I needed cash back and I always kept my accounts in good standing. At this point my credit was immaculate and I didn't do things like this *ever*! My dad came and picked me up and would barely talk to me the entire way. This silence was so tense and awkward, and I was shocked how angry he was with me. I was used to never really having consequences for my actions and this was quite different because now I lived with my family again and was no longer living on my own.

Later that day, JT called me and asked me how long I spent in jail and he told me he got out that day with his attorney. He never brought up what I was arrested for at the hotel. I told him about seeing Kris and how I knew he was the one who wrote the check. I never went back around JT because of the shame and guilt I had. I began chilling with Dayton again, but I still got the dope with Dayton from the same connect JT used. I would always stay in the car so people wouldn't know it was me. It was like a walk of shame every time I pulled up and I did my best to hide my face.

Nearly four months later, I took my little brother's car to go to traffic court in Austin. Afterwards I had to go to my college campus to take an exam. I had a handicap sticker that wasn't mine, but I didn't want to use it and break the law, so I continued searching for a parking spot. I finally found one and was already forty-five minutes late for court. Everything went fine at court, but when I walked outside my little brother's car was gone! I was so stunned this happened! I found out later that they illegally towed the car, and the city of Austin later reimbursed the impound money.

As you can imagine, my parents were fed up with me and my crazy circumstances. All the times it was my fault overshadowed this one time that was not my fault. I only had my purse and cellphone which was nearly dead. I took so much medicine that I had a separate bag for that, and it was in the car along with all my money. I called my parents over and over, but they never came and got me. I kept telling my mom I couldn't just keep talking on the phone because my battery was about to die, and I begged her to come pick me up. Eventually my battery died, and I was stranded. At this point I walked near my campus, which was in the middle of a crack infested neighborhood. A man bought me some cigarettes and I hung out with random people who gave me some free crack. I wanted to get high, but I never got high in public, so I gave the dope away.

I got up and started walking to the store up the street. My body was hurting from the Fibromyalgia and I had no medicine in my purse. At this point I had been stranded for over twelve hours. A guy at the gas station offered to help me and bought me some water and a Twix bar. I told him I had no money on me, but I could pay him back as soon as I got my car out of the impound. I was dressed nice and didn't look like I was an addict. I was hopeful that he would do just as he said, and I would be okay.

When we began riding to the northside of Austin, I started to get nervous and I was wondering where we were going. I should've just used someone's phone to call Mrs. Jones, but I had put her through so much already, and didn't even think of it until it was too late! We pulled into a hotel parking lot and I waited in the car while he paid for a room. This was the same hotel that I had been arrested at almost four months earlier, so I tried to keep a low profile. He came back in the car and said that he got me a room, but he would not be staying. I walked in the room and at once turned on sports hoping to distract him from me. I laid down and immediately fell asleep.

The next thing I know he jerked me on to my back and said, "B**CH, you gonna give me some of this pu**y!" The man I was looking at didn't look anything like the calm man I met, and I still don't remember anything past those vulgar words he said to me. The next memory I have is hearing water running, but I never woke up. When I awoke, I was alone, and my clothes were covered in blood and I was in pain. I was terrified and had no idea what to do. I almost went to the hotel office, but I thought they would take me to jail for violating the trespassing warrant. I knew if I could just tell them which room, I was in then they would have his identity, but I couldn't risk going to jail. I still don't know if I was drugged or just disassociated, either way I can't remember.

I was in complete shock and wandered around Austin trying to get my head together. I had never taken the city bus, plus I had no money to ride it anyway. Someone on the street helped me get in contact with my mom and she was supposed to meet me at my college. She wired me money for a cab, but I spent it on clothes at Walmart. I smelled horrible and was scared I had contracted something from this guy. It took me a couple trips to Walmart to get everything I needed because I was so confused. I had no concept of time and eventually made it to my college campus. I went and told them what happened and showed them my bloody clothes. They offered to give me my $500.00 refund check a week early. I went to see the counselor and she called my mom and I remember screaming at my mom. I was so angry that she left me. She said she had been there to get me, but I never showed up, but I was still angry she never came before I was even raped.

I took the $500.00 check my school gave me and got a hotel room. I bought crack with most of the money and had people in my hotel room. I was so upset I wasn't even smoking it. I gave nearly all of it away then laid there watching the Golden Girls thinking about Grammy. She had been gone four years now. I ended up getting kicked out of that hotel for having homeless people in it, so I wondered the streets and met a guy. I chilled with him awhile and would see people in the street I knew back when I thought I was on top of the world. I had hit bottom but not rock bottom. I smoked crack with the guy I had just met but mostly would just lay there. He was an addict, but he was a decent guy. He rode the bus with me to the hospital since I didn't know how to take the bus. The rape advocate at the hospital tried to get me to do a rape kit and go after the rapist and she assured me they would help support me. I thought about how my mom reacted with Cash and replied that I didn't have the family support necessary to endure court proceedings. I got checked for STD's and once I got my negative results, Pastor Jones picked me up and drove me forty-five miles to my parent's house.

I was supposed to start counseling at my college campus the following Monday, but I never returned to college. It was hard enough managing Fibromyalgia, trauma from my childhood, addiction, but now another rape? I gave up! I was in my senior year nearing the completion of my bachelor's degree and just gave up. I remember thinking, "I will just come back, better to finish strong than barely make it!

Chapter XIX

And shed innocent blood,
The blood of their sons and daughters,
Whom they sacrificed to the idols of Canaan;
And the land was polluted with
blood. – Psalm 106:38

About this time, I transitioned from crack to meth. I had never done meth, but I tried it after getting stranded somewhere selling pills. Within a month of trying meth I began shooting it up. The meth scene opened a world of darkness I could have never dreamed existed. The whole meth culture is crazy, and I couldn't stand it, but I dealt with it. They single people out to intentionally make them go crazy and just laugh at them. They steal your stuff and try to help you find it. People would get high and go look for "shadow people." The things and the culture of the meth community is extremely demonic. Within a couple of months, I began spending most of my time staying with this married couple at their house. There were always people there and I had yet to become addicted to meth, so I would stay in the living room while everyone would be in the bedroom getting high.

I wanted to sleep and be alone more than anything and would often let them take my car in exchange for staying at their house. I had full coverage insurance, but I did not have a home, so it was worth it to me!

Within a couple of months of staying at their house I found out I was pregnant. I was thinking it was impossible for me to be pregnant because I was not active with anybody. I went to a restaurant one day and a woman approached me to tell me that her husband confessed to drugging me and raping me with two other men. One of the men she named was the husband of the married couple I was living with and another man she named was someone I thought was my friend. He would come over to the married couple's house a lot, and we had become friends. I still have no memory of any of it, except I remember waking up on the bedroom floor one day, when I always slept on the couch. That is all I can remember. Around twelve weeks, I decided to get an abortion. I received a phone call one day from my ex, Kris. He was in the county jail where I lived, and he told me that there were three men there claiming to be the possible father of my baby. I asked him what their names were, and he named the same three men that the girl told me at the restaurant. I went on to tell him that there was no baby and that I already had an abortion. As much as I hated it, the confirmation coming from someone who was from out of state, made what happened a bit more concrete, although I still have no memory.

Following the abortion, my soul grew more caged and darker. I don't see how I ever thought abortion was okay for a mother to do, even following the act of rape. Can you imagine having a limb amputated and suffer no emotional or mental repercussions? That's what I expected after amputating my own child from my womb. I didn't need another child because my mom was raising the two children I already had, but looking back, adoption would've been a much better solution. I definitely didn't realize that a spirit of death would follow me for many years to come because of it. Whether I agreed at the time or not, abortion was and is murder! I later learned how this same act was carried out as a sacrifice to false gods by some of the people in the Bible, and that Jesus was and will always be 100% against abortion! Satan has been deceiving the masses into thinking abortion is normal and okay. Many of the people he deceives are Christians.

A few weeks after the abortion I went for the follow-up appointment. My mom took me, and we planned to swing by my lawyer's office to pick up a substantial check I was to receive for a car wreck I was in the year before. Kris and I were in a car accident and got rear ended by a company vehicle. We both were compensated $8000 each. On the way to the lawyer's office, she was telling me that my dad wanted me to turn myself in for the warrant I had for missing court. I told her that my dad would never say that and not to lie to me. Before the appointment we went to Applebee's and she let me order shots of Patron, which was not like her at all. She joked that it would come out of my check.

We left to go to the appointment and after picking up my two checks, $4000 each, I fell asleep on the way home. I felt the car jerk and I quickly awoke demanding to know why she would drive like that if I had a warrant. The next thing I saw was the Sherriff Department behind us pulling my mom over. The officer came to my side immediately and told me to get out of the car. I told him one second and reached for a bottle of pills I already had made for when I'd have to go to jail. I wanted to be able to sleep through it and not be pacing around. I took the pills and reached for some tea, but the tea was empty. I had to swallow the pills with no liquid. My mom made a nervous laugh and said something like, "Oh that's my daughter always taking pills." I started to get out of the car and my mom was crying. I assured her it would be okay and to just bond me out and reminded her of what to do. We had been through this dozens of times. In an instant her tears dried, and she said, "Here, sign your checks so I can come get you." My bond was only a few hundred dollars. She had me sign both $4000 checks and I got out of the car.

When I got to jail, I started putting everything together from what she said about my dad, allowing me to get drunk, the police behind us, and the checks. I knew at that moment that my mom set me up to get the money. What hurt me wasn't just that I was on my way home from an abortion check-up, but I already planned to give her and my dad $1,500 each. I felt betrayed and any trust or respect I had for her was gone! I would carry unforgiveness and bitterness toward her for many years. This also affected my credit, and it went from exceptional to me being sued because I planned to use the money from the car wreck to pay off small loans that I got to build my credit. This was my last resort to pay for those things which made me very angry. I told my mom to hold on to the money because I obviously had a drug problem and just give me money for gas and to pay the loans off for me. She gave me $500 in cash and the next time I called her for gas money she said it was all gone! None of my loans got paid off and I only saw $500 out of $8000. This would be another scene Satan would replay in my mind over and over.

Chapter XX

The lamp of the body is the eye. Therefore, when your eye is good, your whole body also is full of light. But when your eye is bad, your body also is full of darkness. – Luke 11:34

During the next two years I was in heavy meth addiction and would find myself nearly killed many times from suffocation attempts, guns to my head, being held against my will, being poisoned, knocked unconscious and left for dead, and many other things. The darkness that covers the meth world is unlike any darkness I had ever known. The people were sick, and I was able to see things that terrified me. I would often begin screaming about the baby I murdered and about the men who raped me. I tried telling the police, but nobody believed me, and I was not mentally fit to endure any court proceedings. I learned as a teenager that nobody would support me going up against a rapist, so I just continued to get high. I walked around with a piece of paper that I wrote "MURDERER" on in big bold letters. I would meditate on this the way I would later meditate on scriptures from the Bible.

During this time, I had warrants for my arrest and was about to pull into some apartments to pick up this guy, but he was outside hemmed up with cuffs on. So, I swung my car around and made a U-turn and rode out to the country in fear that I may be connected to the reason he was being arrested. I went to this other guy's house I had been to a few times before with other people. He lived on his own property and I knew that would call for a different type of warrant if the police showed up, and I hadn't done anything that bad to get a search warrant for private property. I went there to gather my thoughts and formulate a plan. I had a lot of valuables with me, because my parents were recently out of town and the guy that had just been arrested had seen the inside of my parents' house so I brought the valuables, mostly jewelry, with me to keep him from sending people into the house to rob it. Apparently, the guy who was cuffed, previously told the people at the property I was sitting on about my valuables.

I was pretty high on meth, but suddenly, the Holy Spirit quickened me and showed me I was being set up. I got sober instantly and He began showing me each person and their intent. One of them was at the back of my Trailblazer messing with the lock on the back hatch, the other one was asking me to come smoke meth inside. When I said no, they began trying to think of other things to offer me. It was clear what was happening. I also knew supernaturally I had to leave. There is no doubt that I was not only going to be robbed but raped. I told them all I suddenly had a terrible feeling in my stomach like somebody died or something bad happened, hinting that I knew what they were doing. I told them when the feeling leaves, I will get out of my car, but until then, I was not moving. A few weeks prior I had a gun put to my head at this same place, so I knew these people loved guns and loved scaring people with them.

When they saw I wouldn't leave my car, they all went inside except one girl. I went and sat in her truck which was next to my vehicle and told her, "I know what y'all are doing and what you have planned." She played dumb and I asked her which way was the quickest way to San Antonio, with the intent of going the opposite way. She told me to turn left at the light and stay straight until I got to San Antonio. I told her that God showed me exactly what was going on and He would help me escape. I told her if she doesn't have anything to do with it then to sit in her truck and give me a minute or two head start. I got in my car and hauled as fast as I could down the country road in the opposite direction that she told me.

The Holy Spirit told me to pull off to a side road that branched off the road I was already on and cut my lights off... so I did. As I slowed down, I heard something rolling on the roof of my car. It didn't fall because I had a rack on the top. When I got out, I saw a screwdriver on the top of my car that those guys had left there. I stayed there for a few minutes and was trying to find which way to go. My gas tank was on E and I knew I wasn't likely to make it home. I decided to go right at the light which was further away from my house and stop at another guy's house. I took all my valuables inside and began telling him what was going on, but when I sat down, I felt even more uneasy. I decided to leave right away. I then remembered he was very close friends with the guys I was running from. I immediately got in my car and left. At the traffic light, two guys from the property were there standing outside their truck waiting for me. It was around 4:00AM. When I saw them, I made a right and went full speed on the road that connected the town I was in, to the town I lived in. They jumped in their truck and began chasing me down a seven-mile country road. I was going the maximum speed, pedal all the way to the ground, trying my best maneuver through the twisting roads of the hill country.

When I got into my town, I was doing over eighty miles per hour in a thirty-five miles per hour speed zone, praying as I ran every light and stop sign that I didn't hit anyone. They were going just as fast and when I got to the gated community I lived in, I yelled at the sleepy guard that the guys behind me had guns and not to let them in because they were not with me. I wasn't sure what the guard would do, but I didn't want the guys to follow me in and say they were with me and be allowed in. I had no idea how close they were behind me because it was dark, and I could only see lights for the most part. It was dangerous to continue looking back at the speed I was driving. The last time I clearly saw the truck behind me we were about 800 feet from the guard gate to enter the gated community. As soon as I pulled in my driveway my car was out of gas. It coasted up to the door because it was empty. I ran up to my door and was banging on it for my dad to unlock it. He thought I was just high, but I was sober as I could be. A couple of months later I ran into both guys at another house. They looked so scared because I was with someone that was feared by people because of his insane rages and huge size. They did not say a word to me when I confronted them about that day. They were silent! I never had a problem out of them again.

I was living with my mom and she told me if I left, I wasn't coming back. I left anyway because I wanted to get high. When I came back, she kept her word and wouldn't let me in. My mom kicked me out and with nowhere to go, so I went back to the dope house I was getting high at. I woke up to the blade of a knife in my back cutting through the top layers of my flesh. This random guy had a knife carving into my back. I pretended not to be scared because I knew that he was checking for fear, and in order to survive I couldn't show any at all! The guy apparently liked it because it showed him that I was as crazy as he was. A lot of dark and twisted associations between sex, drugs, and pain began taking root in the months that followed. I would go further into darkness in this area as well and it took the power of the Holy Spirit and lots of scripture to deprogram the associations that had been set up in my soul.

I stayed at the dope house and the guy was also there. Often it was just me and him in the house and we just began to spend a lot of time together. Eventually we both left the dope house and went to stay with his mom. On one occasion I was trying to go home but he had my car rigged where I couldn't get in it without him. I tried to wake him up and he woke up and threw me on the bed and began suffocating me with a pillow. I was only 115 pounds and he weighed 350. The bed broke and fell three feet to the ground with his weight on top of me. His mom overheard, came in, and told him to get off me or she was calling the police. He got off me and I went home. The next day I had black and blue bruises all over my face, under my eyes, on my lower back up to my midback, and on my butt. I still deal with the injuries from the impact of the bed collapsing. Despite this happening I still went back to get high. I lived in my car there at his mom's house because after the bed incident, his parents wouldn't let me come inside. Over the course of a couple days, he would constantly be in fits of random rage.

He charged at my car and nearly ripped the doors off the hinges and broke the windows.

He destroyed the car with his bare hands until it was totaled. Once he messed my car up, his rage was directed towards me. He shoved my head down toward the ground which caused a neck injury that terrified me. I feared he would kill me if I stayed. I ran to the nearby dollar store and finally called my dad. My dad came to pick me up and that forced me to stay at my mom's house. I would often leave for periods of time, but I tried to be better about calling or would just get high and stay home.

During this time, I began to have weird sensations in my head. I would shake my head and it would stop, but then it would happen again. I was sharing a room with my uncle that was visiting and he said that I was pretending to cry. When he asked me what was wrong, I began laughing in a demonic voice. This scared him so much, he was ready to stay in a hotel to get out of the room with me. These sensations continued to happen until one night I began yelling in a demonic voice, "RUN!" It was the middle of the night. My grandparents and uncle were visiting, and I was sleeping in the living room. I somehow got into a chair outside on the porch and began spinning around in the chair while yelling, "RUN!" Next thing I remember is being on the living room floor trying with all my strength to get on the air mattress, but I couldn't lift myself off the floor. I was continuing to yell in a demonic voice, "RUN!" My grandma, grandpa, uncle, and dad came out, and I could see the sheer terror in their eyes. My grandma began praying and my grandpa asked if I needed a priest. I remember trying to communicate to my grandma that I needed help, but I couldn't speak. I tried hard to communicate with my eyes to my grandma who showed no fear as she walked toward me praying. I was aware the entire time of what was happening, but I couldn't stop it!

My dad called the ambulance, and I was so scared because I didn't want to get put away in a mental hospital for good. Right before the ambulance got there it stopped, and I was able to shake my head no. I told them I didn't want to go to the hospital and that I just had a headache. My dad was worried because I had suffered numerous head injuries and would often have symptoms of post-concussion syndrome, but I knew this wasn't that! I remember my son asking me one day, "Mommy, why do your eyes look like reptiles?" I shuddered at the thought of my eyes looking like a snake, because I was so terrified of them to the point that I recently had to go through deliverance in this area. I recently saw a picture of me from a few years ago and assuredly, one of my eyes clearly looked like a snake. I later learned demons often manifest through people's eyes.

A few days later I was eating breakfast and in severe pain screamed, "Ahhhhh!" My family all got worried and called the ambulance again thinking I had an aneurysm or something. I went to the hospital and everything was fine, and I returned home. I never had those sensations again, but years later I learned that demons often leave out of the head and many times its very painful! There is no doubt that God once again intervened on my behalf and vacated whatever was trying to take over my body completely!

Another day, I was hanging at some apartments and I had just been shooting meth when a girl tried to fight me over a guy, and it escalated to the police being called. I took off running from some apartments and I began running in a creek that was much deeper than I thought. The next thing I knew, it was no longer dark, the sun was shining, and I woke up in water up to my neck about a half mile in the water from where I started. I have no memory of how I got there. I have no idea how I fell asleep in water after shooting meth, but I'm thankful I didn't die. When I woke up, I was completely sober and that was odd because one dose usually stuck with me for three to four days.

Chapter XXI

Grace to you and peace from God the Father and our Lord Jesus Christ, who gave Himself for our sins, that He might deliver us from this present evil age, according to the will of our God and Father. – Galatians 1:3-4

The whole family went together to a family function about six hours away. Mike came to visit, and every time Mike came around, I was emotionally triggered from my childhood, but I was silenced because my family was tired of hearing it. I often felt like Mike was the loved and cherished child and I was the rejected insane child. The feelings of rejection were always stronger around my brother. I kept it cool and held all my feelings inside during the trip, but when I got back to my mom's house, in an effort to release everything pent up, I cut my arm with a knife, wrapped it up, and was going to leave to go for a walk. Before I could leave, my family called the ambulance, and they took me to a hospital.

When I got there, they gave me a local anesthetic to numb the area, and they stitched up the cut. I was waiting to be evaluated for release, and the woman was taking a while, so I got up to go outside and go sit on the bench. Before I could get outside, the nurse and security chased me down to stop me. Security approached me and immediately put my arm behind my back, causing me to stumble and I fell backwards on my arm. They took me for x-rays and found it wasn't broken, although my shoulder remained in pain for the next five years. Sadly, they even released me in this state to myself after being instructed not to release me until my parents were there for me since I was a threat to myself. My mom firmly warned them not to let me go without her there. When they released me, they had no idea whether anyone was there or not. My mom had no idea I was released or where I was. When I got released, I called a friend to pick me up. When my mom got to the hospital to pick me up, I was already gone, and they had no record of where I was. There were so many system failures, but I would continue paying for it, as is the case with so many within the criminal and mental health system. It's just a broken system that's overworked and underpaid. I could have been a casualty of this broken system, but again, God showed me mercy and I was able to get help, for which I was thankful!

I was released from the hospital and returned later that day with my mom, after reconnecting, so I could be transported by the sheriff to the MHMR (Mental Health Mental Retardation) crisis center. When my mom called MHMR they told her I had called the week before and was trying to get help, but they hadn't contacted me yet. I was getting tired of this life and was trying to get out! I was sent to a crisis center for thirty-four days while awaiting a bed in a rehab. I loved the crisis center and had peace and enjoyed being clean and sober. The hospital pressed charges on me nearly thirty days after they discharged me. They claimed I assaulted one of the nurses. This was an attempt to keep me from suing the hospital.

Although I wasn't guilty for this charge, I agreed to get help and received my second PR (Personal Recognizance) bond in place of the required $50,000 bond. The crisis center had a relationship with criminal court system and if I agreed to follow through with going to rehab, they could get me a PR bond. This way I wouldn't have to pay any money and I wouldn't have to sit in jail. I was supposed to be in rehab for thirty days, but I only stayed for three weeks because they were over prescribing me Xanax to the point I couldn't function. The only way to not be in violation of refusing my medication was to get it adjusted by my medical doctor, so I left the program. Instead of going back they offered me an opportunity to finish in an outpatient program that would start a few months later. When I got out of rehab, I was still abusing the pills I was prescribed, but I virtually stopped meth.

God promises that we overcome by the blood of the Lamb and the word of our testimony (Revelations 12:11). I feel freer than when I began writing the book and I believe I need to be honest. Through word of mouth I found out this man's wife was messing with my ex, Kris. I reconnected with her husband because we had been friends a few years before. I would see and spend time with him here and there, but it wasn't serious. There was no commitment. I only saw him on occasion, but I ended up pregnant again. I think I was halfway getting back at his wife for allegedly being with Kris, but regardless I was wrong! I was terrified to cause people close to me more shame, and again I feared man more than God. I cared more about other people's reputation than doing what was right. I'm not sure his wife ever knew. I was hoping someone would encourage me to keep the baby, but nobody did. My mom was already raising my two kids and pressing for me to get an abortion and the married man didn't want me to keep it either, so I went ahead and aborted the baby. The guilt of the two abortions weighed on me more than I ever knew but God would later open a door for healing to occur.

I can imagine if someone is reading this they may be thinking, "Wow! She just doesn't stop!" Especially if they are religious and perhaps don't come from the type of life I do. However, I can confidently say that I'm the type of woman Jesus died for. His blood purchased me before I would ever commit any of the sins that I have openly shared with you. My prayer is that all people would come to the knowledge of Jesus Christ and to the awareness of their need for Him. Many times, it is the worst sinners that end up having a real intimate relationship with Jesus because the religious folks are content in their day to day activities and have never really acknowledged their own depravity and sickness.

In the Bible there is a story found in Luke chapter seven that I've come to appreciate even more as I see it being played out in my own life. This is where the sinful woman came to the house of the religious people where Jesus was eating. This woman, who was known as a sinner came with an alabaster flask of fragrant oil. She began washing Jesus' feet with her tears and wiped them with her own hair before kissing and anointing them with fragrant oil. The religious people were going crazy seeing this sinner touching Jesus and Jesus not sending her away. Jesus went on to tell Simon a story about two debtors. One of the debtors owed 500 denarii and the other only fifty denarii. They were both forgiven when they both were unable to pay their debt. Jesus asked Simon, "Tell me therefore, which of them will love him more?" (Luke 7:42) In the next verse Simon replied, "I suppose the one whom he forgave more." Jesus goes on to tell Simon he indeed was correct. Jesus goes onto say "Therefore I say to you, her sins, which are many, are forgiven, for she loved much. But to whom little is forgiven, the same loves little (Luke 7:47)."

The love and devotion that come from followers of Jesus that have lived truly wretched lives will often surpass the love of religious or well-to-do people, for we have truly seen our state apart from Christ. This same level of love and gratitude for our own forgiveness empowers us to forgive the most unforgivable sins committed by others; either against us or humanity. People who have been forgiven much will love other people, especially the ones that are hard to love!

Chapter XXII

while it is said: "Today, if you will hear His voice, Do not harden your hearts as in the rebellion." – Hebrews 3:15

In the spring of 2014, I began the Intensive Outpatient Program (I.O.P). I enjoyed going to the program and did better at staying clean from meth. I still had a prescription for pain pills and Xanax. One day I was in the I.O.P class and I heard the Holy Spirit say, "Look up My promises." I wrote it down on a post-it note and put it in my folder. I kept forgetting to look them up, but He would remind me. One day an old friend from Florida posted a promise on Facebook from a website called 365Promises.com. I went to the website and signed up for a daily promise to be emailed to me. I also began writing scriptures on flashcards and placing them around my house. I often would watch Joyce Meyer and I would write down all the scriptures she would teach on, then after the show I would go write them down on flashcards too! I still practice writing scriptures on flashcards today! I continued making progress slowly but surely.

During my alone time with God, weeping in tears, I asked God to pour His love in my heart. I could not feel love for anyone, nor could I receive it. I was entirely numb! I had a vision of the depressed care bear with the cloud on his stomach above me in my room, and a rainbow shot out of him and into my heart. I physically felt God's love break the hardness of my heart and I began weeping and crying because suddenly I could finally *feel* love… and even godly sorrow was increased exponentially! Not a sorrow that just made me feel bad, but a sorrow that produced change. I began holding pictures of people I hurt and crying intensely for how I treated them. I would pray for those who hurt me and would see a vision of a sledgehammer breaking down a fortress of bitterness, hate, and unforgiveness around my heart that kept me separated from the presence of God. It's interesting that I never even considered that I was being a hypocrite. I'd pour my tears out to God for what was done to me and He would comfort me, but He also lifted the veil of self-deception that was covering my own sin and hypocrisy. I've gone through deep repentance and cried out from the depths of my inner most being, but this time, not for what was done to me, but what I had done to others.

A couple of years earlier I walk-ed into a library after injecting meth and they were giving free spiritual books away. I took some and stored them in my closet and had forgot about them. One day I was reminded of the books and began pulling them down from the shelf in my closet. I chose a book called *Grace Walk*. It even had a study guide in the back, and I would spend hours in my room reading and doing the study. I was determined to understand God's grace and how I was covered by the blood of Jesus. I had the hardest time trying to comprehend the grace of God.

Some people speak poorly of TV pastors because of "hyper-grace," but I am thankful because I needed it drilled in my head. I remember watching Creflo Dollar one day and it all clicked. In time God began moving me on to other pastors, but there is no doubt those on TV are effective in helping people understand the grace of God and what it means to be in Christ.

The Holy Spirit also reminded me of a book that I was given around 2008 at my old church. It was a red prayer book with doves on it. I remembered I gave it away to someone that I thought needed it more than me; I told you I was deceived. I couldn't figure out how to find the name of it, but the Holy Spirit gave me the idea of looking it up in the app store and there it was! I began sitting outside and praying the prayers for hours every day. I also still practice this daily, if not that prayer book then another prayer resource. I love that prayer book and I later found out it is in many jails and prisons and has helped countless people!

Things began to move quickly, and I was forced to get off Xanax after my doctor was indicted on criminal charges and lost his license, which made all my refills invalid. I knew it was God helping me and I chose not to find another doctor. I continued getting pain pills at pain management and was also getting Klonopin. I was terrified of being sober, but God helped me, and I had to choose to remain in the help He provided.

One day as I was standing in the garage, I heard God's voice again just like the day in the furniture store nearly ten years earlier. This voice was different than the still small voice and I can only remember hearing it four or five times my entire life, but it always got my attention and I always obeyed! As I was standing in the garage everything looked gray and dreary. I wondered, "Will my life ever be how it used to be?" Let me remind you when I first came to Jesus, I had a lot of trauma, but nowhere near the amount I carried after all the things that happened because of my rebellion and addiction. I didn't say it aloud, but God knows our heart and our mind.

He responded, "Do you want what I have for you or not?"

I responded, "Yes, Lord!"

Instantly I knew I had to get off the pain pills, and I was willing even with the pain I had, to give them up. Within about a week, my friend who worked at the pain management clinic called me saying, "I'm sorry chica, but we don't take your insurance anymore, you'll have to go somewhere else." I assured her she shouldn't be sorry, and that God was helping me get off the pills! At the same time my dad's pain management doctor moved abruptly and my dad was also off his pills that he took because of a broken neck. My dad and I detoxed together and we both felt better after the withdrawal symptoms passed. I was taken off Oxycodone, Dilaudid, Morphine, and Klonopin nearly overnight! We were both so happy to get off the pills even though we both had legitimate reasons for taking them, we were getting our life back!

During this time, I would spend hours with God praying and reading the Bible or the red prayer book. I was really seeking Him for who He was for the first time. I was not completely clean and sober yet, but He was working and taking one thing away at a time. Looking back, I realize that this entire time I had been wrong about why God brought me back to my mom's house. I thought I was sent there to be punished, but in all actuality, He brought me there to heal me. Scripture says, "Therefore behold, I will allure her, Will bring her into the wilderness, and speak comfort to her. I will give her vineyards from there, And the Valley of Achor as a door of hope; She shall sing there, As in the days of her youth, As in the day when she came up from the land of Egypt" (Hosea 2:14-15).

Looking back, I wish I wouldn't have waited so many years to finally surrender it all. God had a good plan for me from the beginning, but I was terrified to have a life without drugs! I'm so thankful for all His help, love, and mercy!

Chapter XXIII

*bearing with one another, and forgiving
one another, if anyone has a complaint
against another; even as Christ forgave you,
so you also must do. – Colossians 3:13*

During this time, I learned of a music ministry called Kingdom Muzic. God used brother Bryann Trejo's testimony of how he had to forgive the people who murdered his identical twin brother and the freedom that forgiveness brought. He began planting seeds in my heart to forgive those who hurt me. Shortly after I discovered Bryann Trejo, I began learning about the things that had to be dealt with in order to be healed and the legal grounds in the spirit realm. I then knew the Fibromyalgia, addiction, and trauma couldn't be healed until I forgave those who hurt me. For an entire year I played this song called, "Love 'Em Anyways."

I continued praying for those who hurt me and listening to that song. After a year God brought my family friend who I held resentment toward back into my life and I was terrified! I had nearly stopped meth and was off all pills except for bipolar, depression, and Fibromyalgia, but none of the pills made you feel intoxicated. When he came back in my life, he was on many hard drugs. During this time God showed me that He healed me of all PTSD symptoms concerning this person, because I could be around this person and not be triggered or feel any symptoms. I was so thankful and amazed! I still had work to do around all the other trauma that took place in my life, but this was certainly a great victory! A month after He brought this person in my life, God started convicting me about smoking marijuana. I heard God's voice again. He said, "You've got to get it together! I need you alert for what's going on. I'm using you to bring your family to Me- If you don't come; they don't come!"

I replied, "Okay Lord."

I knew this time He meant let go of the weed, so I tried many times to stop but was always unsuccessful. I was angry that God was making me get sober first. I told Him, "I feel like your sacrificing me for my family.

He responded, "How do you think my Son felt?"

I agreed to be obedient even though everything in me didn't want to do this. About this time someone on Facebook began posting prayers about breaking curses and renouncing sins. I started copying and pasting the prayers into a digital notebook in an app on my phone. I began praying them all day every day. I began with one prayer and now have about seventy prayers and I have made the folder available to over seventy other people, to the glory of God! I began taking time each day to declare the word of God over me and confessing my identity in Christ! I would google "identity in Christ" or "scripture declarations for peace or anger" etc. I have no doubt those declarations produced change in me supernaturally, because they were 100% based on scripture! His word is alive and active (Hebrews 4:12).

I continue doing declarations every day and it has gone past head knowledge into being weaved into my entire being! Every time God would show me another part of myself that needed to change, I would search for scriptures that would address that and began praying them over myself in faith in Jesus name! I will continue this practice until I go home to be with the Lord Jesus or Jesus returns!

Despite all this deliverance, I had yet to be delivered from a spirit of suicide and death that had followed me since I was a kid. I woke up happy one morning at my mom's house. I got up and while crossing through the living room on the way to the kitchen, I told everybody good morning. My mom cut her eyes at me and said, "We're talking."

I responded, "I should just kill myself."

My dad chimed in, "Go ahead."

I walked out and went straight to my pill bottle and took the pills. After I came to the realization of what I did, I realized I didn't want to die. I thought about the time Mrs. Jones told me the devil can't take me out, but he can trick me into taking myself out. This is exactly what he did, and this speaks to how badly the devil fights you when you're about to breakthrough. I changed my shirt and tried to go outside to call the ambulance because I was embarrassed to tell my family what I had done. Before I got outside, I collapsed and started convulsing. I couldn't believe right as I began to make progress, I ended up in ICU and almost put on life support! Right before they were going to put me on life support my kidneys went from shutting down to working at 150%! I was saved yet again by Jesus Christ! I remember when He spoke to my heart, "You, don't even know what I have for you." I type this with tears as I'm reminded of that day when I felt His love and sadness for me. Although I could only see death and pain, He saw my future. The Bible says, "For I know the thoughts that I think toward you, says the Lord, thoughts of peace and not of evil, to give you a future and a hope" (Jeremiah 29:11). It goes further to say, "Then you will call upon Me, and I will listen to you. And you will seek Me and find Me, when you search for Me with all your heart" (Jeremiah 29:12-13).

Chapter XXIV

Repent therefore and be converted, that your sins may be blotted out, so that times of refreshing may come from the presence of the Lord. – Acts 3:19

When I got home, the Holy Spirit began opening my eyes to the spiritual war. He showed me that the spirit of death and suicide worked with the spirits that operated through my family. When I was on the floor, before the ambulance came and I was gasping for air, having seizures, and going in and out of consciousness, I'd see my parents just staring and mocking me. I was upset about this until God took me back to this and showed me those weren't my parents at that moment but were demons manifesting. "For we do not wrestle against flesh and blood, but against principalities, against powers, against the rulers of darkness of this age, against spiritual hosts of wickedness in heavenly places" (Ephesians 6:12). As I would pray these warfare prayers, God gave me revelation and understanding of what I was doing and how it was all connected.

Months later, I fell again into meth and this time shot up, which I had just began doing after a couple years of stopping that. I noticed I couldn't get high and I was still able to eat and everything which was abnormal! There was this girl who lived up the street and we would get high together. I began shooting up at my house and I called her to go to her house because I didn't want my family to know I was high. When I got to her house, I went into her bathroom to shoot more and I heard the Holy Spirit clearly say, "Throw it away and the chain is broke!" I immediately flushed it with no hesitation! I walked out the bathroom and went to go sit back down next to the girl whose house I was at. At that moment I came under heavy warfare and demons started speaking through her. She would begin bringing up how this girl was raped, knowing that it triggered the past abuse of my life and it started sending me into a state of PTSD which distorted my perception and caused sensory overload. This wasn't the first time she'd bring up the same story about the girl being raped, and she would watch me dissociate, which is why I knew she understood what she was doing. I ended up leaving her bedroom and going into the living room with her son. I could hear demonic voices behind the cartoons that her son was watching and behind the video games. I had been on drugs most my life, but I had never heard these voices. I tried praying and repenting, but my tongue was bound, and I couldn't speak. I went in her son's room to be alone and I focused as hard as I could through the PTSD symptoms so I could send a text message to someone and ask them to call me on the phone and pray for me. They called me immediately and I walked outside. As they began praying, I began saying, "J-J-J-JESUS!"

I walked back inside talking and the girl who was there said, "What happened I thought you couldn't talk?"

I said, "I couldn't but someone prayed and now I can!"

Her mouth dropped open, because she was an atheist.

Once I was able to get a ride home from her house, my life would be forever changed! As I was sitting in the chair in my living room, I began seeing a light shining. I got up and checked for car headlights and saw nothing. I repeated this a few times. During this time, I was communicating with God through scriptures like a phone conversation! He would say something, and I had a reply that went like a conversation, but it was all scripture. It was amazing! Many of the scriptures I didn't know but He gave me grace at that moment to commune back and forth with Him through His Holy Spirit.

I realized the light was getting brighter and looked down and saw it was coming out of my chest. I was literally glowing with light! I later learned the following verse which is exactly what I was experiencing, "So shall they fear the name of the Lord from the west, and His glory from the rising of the sun. When the enemy shall come in like a flood, the Spirit of the Lord shall lift up a standard against him" (Isaiah 59:19).

I was witnessing this verse with my own eyes and I was wide awake, not sleeping or dreaming! After this, I began hearing heavenly music and received my first assignment. I wrote everything down in a notebook as it was happening. I have no idea how long all this lasted, but I believe it was at least two days, based on my dad asking me had I eaten or had I been to sleep yet. God was showing me all the times He was with me and He was showing me my calling.

"Or do you despise the riches of His goodness, forbearance, and longsuffering, not knowing that the goodness of God leads you to repentance?" (Romans 2:4). I know that it was the goodness of God that led me to truly repent! When I first came to Christ in 2007, I wanted Jesus, but I was not willing to truly repent and turn from my sin; now I was, and my actions proved it! "So produce fruit that is consistent with repentance [demonstrating new behavior that proves a change of heart, and a conscious decision to turn away from sin] (Matthew 3:8 AMP). This is what I missed the first time; fruit or actions that testified that my heart had been changed and I no longer viewed sin as being okay. I was hurt before and knew I had done wrong in life, but I wasn't truly repentant. I was still consumed with seeing myself as the victim and never realizing my own need for Jesus!

I began to weep over my sinful state and not just because I had consequences from sin. I truly had godly sorrow over the choices I made in life and how I treated people, and I saw it as God saw it; It was sin! "For godly sorrow produces repentance leading to salvation, not to be regretted; but the sorrow of the world produces death"(2 Corinthians 7:10). My response to God for intervening on my behalf was complete love and devotion, which was evident by my obedience to remain clean! I knew the Spirit of the Lord visited me that day and my deliverance had come, and I would do anything necessary to hold on to it!

So, since that day my desire for drugs has been gone!

When temptation came, I knew I had a choice and didn't have to do it! It was back to being like the first time I began using drugs; it was a choice and not an addiction, I was taken back to that place where I had a choice. If your sitting in a jail or prison today, when you get out, you have a choice! You don't have to go back to that life! If you are reading this in a library or in your home, know that you have a choice! Call on God to free you from your bondage, whatever the bondage may be!

Unfortunately, I didn't stop smoking weed until two months after this. In my eyes, I continued smoking for the physical pain, but looking back I can also see boredom and my environment was a reason. I remember when I would smoke weed, I would hear the Holy Spirit say, "I have given you joy and now you are numbing it?" I agreed what I was doing didn't make any sense, because I did have hope and joy and every time I would smoke, I would feel God convicting me, but I would also feel condemned. I knew it wasn't God condemning me, but it was the devil, and I decided the only way to avoid it, was to stop! A sweet sister also encouraged me as I told her I smoked and I really saw nothing wrong with it, she replied, "John 3:30, sis." I went and looked it up and read, "He must increase, but I must decrease." This was John the Baptist speaking saying that he must decrease so Jesus could increase. When I read that I realized it was not about what I wanted to do but God taking precedence in my life. I needed to decrease so Jesus could increase. I went and wrote it on a flashcard and began confessing it out loud and within a couple months, God removed every temptation (people who also smoked weed) in my house and delivered me. When the temptations came back, it was a choice that I had to make to stay off it and I did!

Chapter XXV

*Many are the afflictions of the righteous,
But the Lord delivers him out of
them all. – Psalm 34:19*

God completely healed all my pain; emotional, physical, and mental! He sent a preacher to me that told me of this deliverance channel on YouTube, called 27 Fasting & Prayer & Agapekind Media. At first, I was leery because I was afraid to listen to the woman speaking because her voice scared me. The preacher told me that it was the demons that God wanted to free me from that were in fear and that's why I couldn't stand to listen to the woman's channel. I began listening to the deliverance prayers constantly and I knew they were working. Through the process of deliverance, I got very sick with vomiting and dizziness and the preacher guy would write me in my inbox to check on me.

He said, "How's it going kid?"

I told him how sick I felt but that I was continuing to listen to the prayers.

He said, "Yeah, it's hard, but I'm sure you'll be more careful of opening those doors again."

He was saying because you see what it takes to get this stuff out of you, you won't be so quick to go sin again. Boy, he wasn't lying. Many times, in temptation I'm reminded of how sick I was, and I will refuse to sin knowing the process I went through to get free! I am no longer on or have need for medication for Fibromyalgia, Bipolar, PTSD, or Depression! I'm Free! I have even been delivered of cigarettes and have not smoked one single drag of a vape or cigarette in years! The deliverance of cigarettes came from a revelation the Holy Spirit gave me.

I heard that voice from the furniture store and it said, "Do you want to overcome or not?"

I responded, "Yes, Lord."

He said, "Then look up the word submit…you wrote it on a flashcard, but you never looked it up."

I said, "Oh you meant the dictionary!"

I had already looked up submit in the Bible and had a long drawn out study but knew at the end I didn't find what He was trying to show me. So, I went and looked up the word submit on my phone and clicked the Thesaurus tab and there it was; to submit meant to abide! I received a vision at that moment and saw Jesus standing over me as a taskmaster that was whipping me, then the vision changed to Jesus walking alongside me! He showed me the problem. I viewed submission wrong because of my abusive past and when He says submit, He just wants me to remain in Him. He is here to walk it out with me and help me, and not to be abusive toward me. I have never taken a drag since. Just like the day God's glory (Light) came in my house, I knew my deliverance had arrived; now I must choose to remain walking in it!

It has been over three years since I witnessed the Spirit of God conquering everything that was too hard for me!

Within two months of all this happening, I was used to lead my kids to Jesus, and I even baptized them in my bathtub. We now read the Bible together and pray together! My family respects me as the new creation the Holy Spirit created me to be! Mike told me one day, "I can't believe your kids listen to you!" He saw the way my kids treated me when he would come visit from Florida. We all lived in the same house and they stopped talking to me altogether. I would speak to them and they wouldn't acknowledge me. They would always be in the room with my mom, and I'd be somewhere in the house by myself. If I told my kids to do anything, they'd just laugh, not taking me seriously or they'd look at me with disgust. There was no respect because of how I behaved, but in God's mercy He turned the hearts of my children back toward me.

I tried my whole life to run and God showed me He can deliver us anywhere we are! He purposely brought me back into the place I ran from to face the very giants that held me bound since a child. He gave me the tools and power to overcome! He turned my kid's hearts back toward me and they have wholeheartedly forgiven me! I used to wonder why God waited so long to show up mightily, but I know part of it was my own will had yet to be broken, and I had not yet developed the character needed to stay free from bondage. I know those aren't the only reasons, but those are a couple. I will never understand His ways fully, but I trust Him fully!

Chapter XXVI

Immediately there fell from his eyes something like scales, and he received his sight at once; and he arose and was baptized. – Acts 9:18

God showed me something else. Scripture says that God will prepare a table in the presence of your enemies (Psalm 23:5). He surely did, but then he told me to serve them at that table! I wasn't expecting that, but through my obedience He used me to snatch the soul of my brother, Mike! I remember days my brother would be mocking Jesus and I would want to leave the room or turn my headphones up.

The Holy Spirit rebuked me and said, "Listen to him, he's hurting!"

I was like, "Wow, really? Listen to him mock you?"

The Holy Spirit would tell me to offer to make him food and when I'd throw it together in my flesh wanting it to look ugly, He corrected me and told me to make it pretty. This went on for almost a year, day in and day out. Then in August 2018, Mike nearly died from kidney failure. I went to the hospital to pick him up and heard the Holy Spirit say,

"Is there anything too hard for Me? You're going to sit there and watch Me save your brother the way others watched Me save you!" I saw two mighty angels, one on each side of my car and they went along with the car every step of the way. I was led by the Holy Spirit to pray this simple prayer on the way, "Lord, take his shame!" I arrived at the hospital and picked him up and my only focus was to be loving. We stopped at a burger stand and we were sitting across from one another, eating, when I reached out for his forearms. I placed my hands on him and began saying, "Bro, God's not mad at you! God's not mad for saying you don't believe in Him! Paul didn't believe in Him and Jesus still chose to reveal Himself to Paul!"

My brother began crying and saying, "My shame is gone, my shame is gone!"

He told me that his teeth were healed. They were hollowed inside from grinding and drugs, and in an instant, they were solid, and all the pain left his body! He told me he thought I was full of it when I told him Jesus healed the nerves in my mouth that were dying. I pointed out that in God's mercy and love, the one thing that you doubted He did for me, is what He chose to do for you! That's the love of God! When we left there, I was hoping he would still go to rehab. I mentioned it and he said, "Whatever you say Jesus." I didn't like that he said that, and I thought he was mocking me as if he was calling me Jesus or like I was trying to play God. That's when he told me what happened at the burger stand.

He said, "Sis you had light coming out of your eyes and your facial structure changed and I saw Jesus!" He said, "I saw Jesus in you, that's why I said that, and remember I didn't believe in God and now I do, and I know Jesus lives in my little sister!" Later that day I also baptized Mike in my mom's bathtub with witnesses on video chat. I didn't realize it until later, but I had been praying for God to send His light, because when His light came to me, I changed! Well God did send His Light, He just sent it through me! I'd later learn this is also a scripture found in the Bible.

"Oh, send out Your light and Your truth! Let them lead me; Let them bring me to Your holy hill and to Your tabernacle" (Psalm 43:3). This is the power of God's love and forgiveness! Not only did Satan try to destroy me through abuse and drugs, but he also tried to destroy Mike through struggles that he faced in his own life. God brought full restoration, salvation, and deliverance to me and now to my brother! We have a good relationship now and it's unbelievable to those who knew us before! Only God can heal a heart and make rivers of living water and compassion flow through it.

"But as for you, you meant evil against me, but God meant it for good, in order to bring it about as it is this day, to save many people alive" (Genesis 50:20). Glory to Jesus! He's given me a testimony of healing, forgiveness, redemption, and reconciliation. His patient love transformed me and now I take this message into a women's correctional facility, where He has me serving every week! God is faithful! Thank you, Jesus!

Chapter XXVII

"So, I will restore to you the years that the swarming locusts has eaten, the crawling locust, the consuming locust, and the chewing locust, My great army which I sent among you." - Joel 2:25

My motive for forgiving in the beginning was so that I may be forgiven by Jesus. I discovered a well-spring of life that gushed out living waters that my parched soul desperately needed. Rivers of living water began flowing through my heart, my body, and my mind. Life-giving water that refreshed and cleansed every aspect of my being. Praying for those who hurt me produced a compassion and love for them that I was unable to produce myself. I know this was the Father sharing His heart with me concerning them. He was not mad at them or at me, but yearned to see us operating in love, unity, and peace.

I can remember praying on my back porch during my days of solitude, "Raise me from these ashes Lord! Raise me up in such a way that anyone looking will know it's You and give You all the credit and none to me!" This was a very different person praying than the one from a decade earlier that took credit for everything God did! He had truly changed me by the power of His Spirit! Accountability did something for me that nothing else could. It gave me a tool to change my life; no matter who disagreed or believed! We reap what we sow, and I began sowing truth and ridding myself of denial; denial of my past and the hurt I caused; the denial of addiction and its effects on my family and children.

The relationship with my mom began to get better as I continued to remain obedient to God. At times I would be frustrated it was taking longer than I hoped to be reconciled, but I realized how badly I had hurt her, and my actions were a huge factor in the hardness of her heart. I continue praying for her and serving her in love and humility, while trusting God to heal her and bring us closer. We have a much closer relationship and there is peace among us and I'm grateful she supports what God is doing through me to reach others. My mom has become one of my greatest supporters and I can imagine it was hard for her during those years. I know she always wanted to support me, but she couldn't support the life I was choosing!

Growing up, my younger brother Maxx and I rarely lived in the same house because of our age difference so I would pick him up and take him to the movies or take him places to spend time with him. When I moved back in with my mom, he was in middle school and he saw me high, and he took care of my kids with my mom. He was a victim of everything I put the entire household through. It was also always difficult to bond with him because of our age difference and different personalities. However, the relationships with both of my brothers are better and we continue making progress toward the future and don't talk about the past. I know a lot of the craziness Mike didn't see, because he lived in Florida, but Maxx saw plenty! I know they know God has done a work in my life and I'm looking forward to watching God work in them, just as He works in me!

During this time of refreshing, God led me to apply to volunteer at the local crisis pregnancy center. I had hopes of sharing what abortion did to me with others and hopefully save lives. They asked me if I had ever had an abortion and I told them I had two, but Jesus healed me. A volunteer requirement was that I first take an abortion recovery class, which I agreed. It was during that class that much more healing was made available to me, and I even had a ceremony for the babies and named them. It gave great closure to me and to know if I exalt my sin higher than the blood of Jesus, I have made my sin an idol over Jesus Christ's forgiveness.

One day when I was at the center, a woman commented on how joyful I am and I heard the Holy Spirit say, "When people comment on the level of joy you have, tell them that's the amount of depression I took from you." The scripture says, "To console those who mourn in Zion, To give them beauty for ashes, The oil of joy for mourning, The garment of praise for the spirit of heaviness; That they may be called trees of righteousness, The planting of the LORD, that He may be glorified" (Isaiah 61:3). This was the manifestation of a fulfilled promise! I had been trying to go back to college for over five years, but I had exceeded the Federal legal limit for both student loans and Pell grants. God breathed on the dreams of my past and opened a door for me to finish college. I began working at my first real job and had only been there a few days when I had a dream. In the dream I was at my college crying on my knees telling people they haven't heard the true Gospel of Jesus Christ.

Someone in the dream said, "Come tell us then."

I replied, "You don't understand, there is no money, it's all gone!"

At that moment a student ran after an administrator and snatched a certificate out of his hand. On the certificate it said November 27, 2018. I woke up and knew God was showing me He had paid it a month earlier. I took a day off work and went to register for classes! Since returning I completed the classes needed to graduate with my B.A. in Psychology. I received an A in every class, while working thirty hours per week, taking prophetic equipping classes, leadership classes, and still being committed to Bridges to Life prison ministry! This is all by the grace of God! I can do nothing without Him! I actually nearly quit the prison, but a dear sister in Christ told me, "If you cut anything you should cut your hours at work. God gave you this ministry!" I immediately heard the Holy Spirit say, "No man, having put his hand to the plough, and looking back, is fit for the kingdom of God" (Luke 9:62). That is when I decided to cut my hours from forty hours to thirty hours per week.

In fact, two of the classes He put me in right away were intensive writing classes. I didn't realize it then, but He used it as training ground for the book you are now reading. I had been out of college for nearly a decade and was excited yet terrified to return, but He remained faithful! I would pray for strategies to be released from heaven so that I could complete all my responsibilities and He never let me down! I completed my internship under the chaplain at the prison and graduated May 2020!

A few months before I began working or going to school, He put it on the hearts of a Christian couple to give me their truck. I would not have been able to finish school or get to work without their obedience to God! The gift of the truck was also a blessing because I had been invited to share my testimony in Houston, Texas, but had no car. I was so excited I accepted immediately without consulting God, but I repented for moving ahead of Him. God came through two weeks before I was to be in Houston and blessed me with my own truck! Most of this book is from the outline He gave me to use for my testimony that weekend in Houston. In the book of Exodus, God sends Moses to Pharaoh with a message. "Then the Lord said to Moses, 'Go into Pharaoh and tell him, 'Thus says the Lord God of the Hebrews: Let My people go, that they may serve Me'" (Exodus 9:1). The Holy Spirit revealed to me as I shared this testimony in Houston, that this is what He did for me. He showed me that just as He sent a standard against Pharaoh for the Hebrews, He sent a standard against the spirit of addiction for me! Pharaoh symbolized the spirit of bondage, but in this case, it was addiction. Just as the Hebrews had been slaves, so had I been a slave to sin and addiction. I was now free to worship Him in spirit and in truth (John 4:24)!

God has raised me up in such a way that everyone is giving Him glory and they know this is beyond anything I could've ever done! One year later, on the exact same day that I received the title for the truck that was gifted to me, I was gifted $9000 for the purpose of buying a car for ministry and to expand the territory God had given me. God blessed me with two vehicles over the course of a year. God also put it on my heart to pray for a quiet cabin by the water to write this book and He answered my prayer. As I type this,

I'm overlooking the water in a cottage, where I've spent less than four days writing this book. It's incredible the places God will take you when your obedient and truly surrender your life. I wish I would've surrendered earlier. He has filled me with so much peace, love, and joy that I feel silly for not trusting Him with all my pain. God's purposes have become my greatest aim and passion while allowing my life to be used by Him for the building of His kingdom and for the salvation of many souls!

    I once broke my hand when I hit the guy who totaled my truck in his mouth. He was sitting in my passenger seat and refused to get out of my truck. Once I hit him in his mouth, he started bleeding and he got out. I never went to the hospital for it and it looked deformed. One day, Jesus healed it right before my eyes in 2017 as I was standing at the fridge. I had never even prayed for this because I broke it hitting someone, but in God's mercy, He healed it! I will never forget standing at the fridge and my hand began shaking noticeably and right before my eyes my hand was straightened out! I was also diagnosed by a dentist with blunt mouth trauma and the nerves in my mouth were dying. It's been years and I have yet to lose the teeth that were loose from the trauma of them being hit. I believe God will continue healing me in every place that remains injured in Jesus name! There is a necessity of staying in faith when believing God for healing. My neck was nearly broken, and I had terrible injuries to my back, and God healed me completely in those areas in 2020! God fulfilled His promise two years after I started writing this book during the editing process.

    I had the opportunity to go to a 3-day retreat for my graduation from ministerial classes. The Lord Jesus had been dealing with my heart about getting off a few medications I got on due to immense pain from the injuries. I told Him, "What do you expect me to do?" I hated being on these after getting off at least thirteen medications, but I began taking so much Ibuprofen it was dangerous. The group transitioned into baptisms which I didn't plan to do, because I had been baptized twice before. I heard a teaching on baptism that was unlike any other teaching! I understood I was literally baptized into Jesus' body and I realized if He isn't sick and injured then I don't have to be! I heard God say loud and clear, "Give them up publicly and I will heal you publicly." Just as times before I responded, "Yes, Lord." I began debating if baptism was necessary or could I just give them up and ask for prayer. About that time the speaker said, "There is power in this water!" I knew that was God telling me I had to be baptized again! I signaled to my daughter to bring my backpack purse that had a bottle in there that held a few of each medication so that I'd be ready when they opened it up for anyone not scheduled for baptism. The Lord reminded me of the angel at Bethesda that stirred the water and whoever got in first was healed, so I was expecting a miracle! When it was my turn, I shared with the crowd and the speaker what the Lord's instructions were and I got in the water. Almost immediately my entire body began shaking violently and for a long enough time I wondered what everybody thought of it. It came in two waves that I could feel. I then stopped and was instructed to take the pills under with me but when I came up not have them in my hand signifying the pills and injuries dying with the old man. When I came up, they placed a robe on me and I felt immense pain in my neck, but it was a different pain. This pain was like a hand had been inside the crevices of my neck moving things around and shortly after I was totally pain free! I later recognized my body shaking as the anointing healing me, it was just like when my hand got healed! God indeed healed me and did it publicly just like He said! Glory to God!

Reflection

I remember the days of solitude that encompassed my being in every way. I remember watching my kids go on about their day to day life without me. I remember my children not speaking to me and the hate and disgust that fueled their stares and facial expressions. I remember being so angry with my mom, I was filled with hate and rage toward her, yet she was the one raising my kids and making all my failures right. She spent countless hours with my daughter teaching her to read because I never did! I knew the importance of education, because not only was my mom a teacher, but she poured her life into us and even on our bedroom walls as kids she would make hand-written posters with "VERB- Action word, NOUN- person, place or thing," and so forth. I was so deceived thinking my mom stole my kids from me when she really stepped in and raised them with love and tried to fix all my failures. I remember when my son asked her if he can call her mom, because it was not fair that he did not have one…I lived in the same house during this time. That is how out of it I was!

I have to be clear that anything I wrote about my family or anyone was not to paint them in a bad light but was to show you that we all make mistakes. We all do the best we can with what we have been given; and at the end of the day we must forgive! I know I need their forgiveness much more than anything they need to be forgiven for, and I also know that Jesus forgave me, and I must forgive to be forgiven!

During much of this time my dad was the only one who would still talk to me and I can remember the pain that set deeply in his eyes. I was a shame and embarrassment to my family and not the daughter I was created to be. I had put my dad through so much since I was eleven years old. When I was 14 years old, my dad caught me with a boy in my room and chased him out the house. The boy jumped on his bike and my dad lunged towards him trying to stop him and grabbed the back tire but broke his hand. I look at his hand now and I remember that day, especially when I watch him play his guitar.

Maxx who was baptized with me in 2007 would help raise my kids when he was only in high school. He was a great role model and instilled great values in my children. He would also go on to not believe in God anymore and I know I was a big part of it. I made the name of Jesus unattractive and a mockery by professing Christ yet living in gross darkness. I still believe God will intervene the way He did with me and Mike, but I caused so much damage to so many people and in ways I may never fully know.

The ways I hurt my children are endless. My daughter has seen so much that she has her own testimony of God keeping her and her baby brother safe! There was a time I was fighting with Kris and he wouldn't let me leave the room, so I tried to leave through the window. When my daughter walked in all she saw was her mama about to jump out of a second story apartment window. She was only six years old. Another instance, both children and I were in the back seat, my mom was driving, and my dad was riding shotgun. There was a lot of tension and passive aggressiveness in a conversation we were having, and she was accusing me of being high. She would not stop talking to me and she kept provoking me, so I opened the door while she was driving full speed so I could get away from her. My son's face was full of terror. My daughter swung her arms around him to hold him tighter. My daughter was about ten years old, and my son was about five at the time. With both of my kids witnessing me trying to jump out a moving car, a second story window, the ambulance at my house countless times for attempted suicide, overdoses, and rageful outbursts, I know the trauma I suffered as a child is small compared to the trauma I inflicted on them. Although I have been forgiven, I am often reminded of what I have done and cry in remorse for the pain I've caused. I'm thankful for the relationship I have with them now and I know I do not deserve it!

Oh, how I need the forgiveness of Jesus! I have sinned so greatly against people and yet Jesus died for me; He died for you too! He died for the people that hurt you! I pray that you will call on Jesus and cry out to Him. I pray you will confess your sins to Him and invite Him into your heart; not just to be your Savior but to be your Lord and Master! Allow Him to have complete control over your life and surrender it all to Him! He loves you and cares for you beyond anything you could ever understand. His blood dripped down from His body hanging on a cross after being crucified; yet in Him there was no sin. He was sent to take on the sins of the world, so that we may come back into fellowship with God; He was not just a man, but was also the Son of God, born of a virgin and after dying for our sins, on the third day, He rose from the grave and is seated in the heavenlies, at the right hand of God the Father, in heaven! He desires to bring you healing, wholeness, and salvation but only through Him is it possible! "Jesus answered and said to him, 'Most assuredly, I say

to you, unless one is born again, he cannot see the kingdom of God'" (John 3:3).

"Repent, and let every one of you be baptized in the name of Jesus Christ for the remission of sins; and you shall receive the gift of the Holy Spirit" (Acts 2:38).

"Repent therefore and be converted, that your sins may be blotted out, so that times of refreshing may come from the presence of the Lord," (Acts 3:19).

"That if you confess with your mouth the Lord Jesus and believe in your heart that God has raised Him from the dead, you will be saved" (Romans 10:9).

Resources

God put it on my heart to make a page where I can list the various resources that made such an impact in my life. In addition to website links and their descriptions, I have included some of the actual prayers, declarations, and confessions that helped me overcome. I hope you will continue to pour God's word over yourself, family, and situations. Don't settle for what Satan throws at you. Learn who you are and how to use the weapons Jesus made available for us to walk in perpetual victory! Additional prayers and teaching can be found on each of the contributor's websites.

    I would like to thank D'blessing of Agapekind Media Ministries for allowing me to include a prayer she wrote for those in spiritual or physical prisons. As you read the prayer, receive it for yourself by faith! I am in agreement and believing for your total deliverance in Jesus name. Her ministry was used by God mightily to bring deliverance to my life and I am forever grateful to God for her obedience. Pastor Robert Clancy of Narrow Path Ministries in Perth, Australia has given me permission to list the #1 prayer that I used daily for over two years! I tell you I did my best not to leave my room without doing this prayer, and if I did,

I regretted it and would quickly return or duck off in the bathroom to pray it. I have also included links to Kingdom Muzic, which is how I heard Pastor Bryann Trejo's testimony of love and forgiveness. I will never forget the work the Holy Spirit did in my heart and mind through this powerfully anointed music ministry!

Resource Links

D'Blessing
Pre-recorded Deliverance Prayers & Teaching
Agapekind Media Ministries
https://www.theagapekindministry.org/
https://www.facebook.com/agapekind/
https://www.youtube.com/user/agapekind

Pastor Robert Clancy
Pre-recorded Deliverance Prayers &
Teaching Narrow Path Ministries
https://www.repentancerevival.com/
https://www.facebook.com/RevivalistRobertClancy/
https://www.youtube.com/channel/UC9hDjFXkfauB0qsg9y0rPGA

Pastor Bryann Trejo
Anointed Christian Rap & Preaching
Kingdom Muzic Ministries
www.kingdommuzic.org
https://www.facebook.com/kmfservant
https://www.youtube.com/user/scotthansen8481

Identity in Christ

I am forgiven (Ephesians 1:7).

I am chosen (John 15:16).

I am cleansed from all unrighteousness (1 John 1:9).

I am healed (Isaiah 53:5).

I am blameless (Colossians 1:22).

I am dead to sin, but alive to God in Christ Jesus (Romans 6:11).

I am the apple of God's eye (Psalm 17:8).

I am His treasured possession (Deuteronomy 7:6).

I am favored (Psalm 84:11).

I am anointed (1 John 2:20).

I am born of God (1 John 3:9).

I am a child of God (John 1:12).

I am a joint heir with Christ Jesus (Romans 8:17).

I am a peacemaker (Matthew 5:9).

I am the righteousness of God in Christ Jesus (Matthew 3:9).

I am called according to His purpose (Romans 8:28).

I am set free from the law of sin and death (Romans 8:2).

I am blessed with every spiritual blessing in Christ Jesus (Ephesians 1:3).

I am saved by grace through faith in Christ Jesus (Ephesians 2:8).

I am redeemed from the curse of the law (Galatians 3:13).

I am a saint (Ephesians 2:19).

I am alive in Christ Jesus (Romans 8:10).

I am the light of the world (Matthew 5:14).

I am a new creation (2 Corinthians 5:17).

I am seated with Christ Jesus in heavenly places (Ephesians 2:6).

I am a friend of God (John 15:15).

I am beloved of God (Colossians 3:12).

Morning Protection Prayer

(used with written permission
from Pastor Robert Clancy)

Pray Aloud!

Father in Heaven, in Jesus name, by prayer & faith, I put on Your whole armor that I may stand against the wiles of the devil. I put on Your Helmet of Salvation. Let the same mind be in me that is in Christ Jesus. I put on Your Breastplate of Righteousness; the Righteousness of Christ. I put on the Girdle (Belt) of Truth. Jesus Christ is the Way, the Truth & the Life (John 14:6). He is the Truth, Integrity & the Holiness of God. I put on Your Sandals of the Gospel of Peace. Help us to stand on the solid ground of Jesus. Above all, I put on your Shield of Faith to quench every fiery dart, arrow, spear & missile the enemy shoots our way. Lord, I put on Your precious Sword of the Spirit, Your Holy Word that's alive & powerful, sharper than any two-edged sword; our offensive & defensive weapon (Heb. 4:12).

1. Scripture: Job 1:10 "Have you not made a hedge around him, around his household, & around all that he has on every side? You have blessed the work of his hands, & his possessions have increased in the land."

Prayer: Father in Heaven, In the name of Jesus Christ, I ask you to keep the same hedge of protection around me, my family, my mind, my heart & emotions, as it is written in Job 1:10.

2. Scripture: Psalm 34:7 "The angel of the LORD encampeth round about them that fear HIM, & delivereth them." Psalms 91:11, 12 "For HE shall give HIS angels charge over thee, to keep thee in all thy ways. They shall bear thee up in their hands, lest thou dash thy foot against a stone" (KJV).

Prayer: Father, in Jesus name, I ask You to keep an encampment of Your powerful angels around me twenty-four hours a day.

3. Scripture: Heb. 1:14 "Are they not all ministering spirits sent forth to minister for those who will inherit salvation?"

Prayer: Father, in Jesus name, I ask you to send a host of ministering angels (in addition to the one each believer has), to minister to our hurts, needs, pain and infirmities, strengthening and comfort us in every way.

4. Scripture: Zechariah 2:5 " 'For I,' says the Lord, 'will be a wall of fire all around her, & I will be the glory in her midst.'"

Prayer: Father, I just praise You & thank You that Your glory is my rear guard (Isaiah 52:12 & 58:8). In Jesus name, I ask

You to surround me with Your supernatural wall of fire, to insulate me from any assaults and the schemes of the devil and his cohorts.

5. Scripture: Genesis 15:1 "After these things the word of the LORD came to Abram in a vision, saying, 'Do not be afraid, Abram. I am your shield, your exceedingly great reward'" (Also Psalms. 3:3).

Prayer: Father, in Jesus name, by faith, I claim Your promise to be my shield, my protector and my exceedingly great reward as Father Abraham.

6. Scripture: 2 Corinthians 10:3-5 "For though we walk in the flesh, we do not war according to the flesh. For the weapons of our warfare are not carnal, but mighty in God for pulling down strongholds, casting down arguments & every high thing that exalts itself against the knowledge of God, bringing every thought into captivity to the obedience of Christ." The mind (our thought life) is Satan's playground. The battle to WIN your mind is in verse five.

Prayer: In the Mighty name of Jesus, I command my mind and all my thought life to come under the obedience & captivity to Jesus Christ as it is written in 2 Corinthians 10:5.

7. Scripture: BINDING and LOOSING – (Matthew 16:19) "And I will give you the keys of the kingdom of Heaven,

and whatever you bind on earth will be bound in heaven, & whatever you loose on earth will be loosed in heaven." See also Matthew 18:18.

Prayer: In the name of Jesus Christ, the Name that is above every name and ALL things (Phil. 2:9,10 & Eph. 1:20- 23). I bind up every unclean spirit & assignment coming against me, my children, and family from, by, or through anyone or anything, named or unnamed, known or unknown, seven generations back. In the name of Jesus, I bind up the principalities, powers, rulers of the darkness of this world, spiritual wickedness and hosts in high places, and the prince of power of the air. In Jesus name, I bind up the strongman, the old man, every prince and stronghold, the spirit of anti-Christ, every evil spirit and plague, the spirit of confusion, illusion & delusion.

In Jesus Christ's name, I bind up the spirit of infirmity, sickness, disease, pain, addiction, affliction, calamity, the devourer, the destroyer, the accuser, the deceiver, the corrupter & every spirit of poverty. In the name of Jesus, I bind up the spirit of strife & division, back biting, and gossip, critical and judgmental spirits, spirits of resistance and hindrance, every spirit of retribution, revenge and retaliation, and the lying, seducing, deceiving spirit of deception (1 Tim 4:1,2).

In the name of Jesus, I bind up every root of fear, rejection, doubt, unbelief, discouragement and every deadly "D" from despair to depression, the spirit of pride, rebellion, disobedience, self, ego, independence, unforgiveness, bitterness, lust and the flesh. I command that every foul and wicked spirit is now burned and removed and be cast into the lake of fire and never to return again in Jesus' Name. Amen and Amen!

THE LORD JESUS CHRIST REBUKE YOU, YOU EVIL, UNCLEAN, AND FOUL SPIRITS
(Jude 9, Zechariah 3:2).

— I (your name) LOOSE God's abundant blessings now, in the mighty name of Jesus Christ; Deliverance, freedom and liberation, peace, joy, hope, gladness of heart, love, healing and wholeness, mercy and grace, blessings and favor, restoration of the years that the locusts have eaten, the resurrection power of Jesus Christ, a mighty harvest, and a boldness to witness for Jesus Christ (Joel 2:25). Amen and Amen!

Prayer of Declarations & Decrees from Spiritual & Physical Imprisonment

written by D'Blessing

Teaching to give understanding prior to prayer:

For those who have been imprisoned, whether spiritually or naturally we're asking for the verdict from the Great Judge! We are asking for the verdict of the One who judges the whole earth! We are asking that even by the finished work of Jesus Christ that souls are liberated from imprisonment!

Imprisonment can come from bitterness, hatred, jealousy, unforgiveness, false accusations, darts of envy, betrayal, etc. There are some things we can't *avoid* because they come to us such as jealousy, betrayals, envy and even offenses, but we know by the power and grace of God we are able to *overcome* these things.

There are people who may have gone into spiritual imprisonment because of unforgiveness, offenses or bitterness. These are pretty simple channels in which the enemy can penetrate the heart and bring people into imprisonment.

Before a man or woman is in prison spiritually there is a doorway and one of the most common doorways is unforgiveness and offenses. There are some other pathways that we can't possibly avoid no matter how hard we try, such as false accusations. We see Joseph falsely accused for a crime he didn't commit (Genesis 39). Daniel was thrown into the lion's den for not bowing to the idols and for choosing to stick with God and God only (Daniel 6).

John the Baptist was thrown into prison in connection to what Jezebel wanted and how she orchestrated that plan and finally he was beheaded. Finally, Paul and Silas were thrown into prison for preaching the gospel. Peter was thrown in prison for preaching the gospel. James was imprisoned and then beheaded for preaching the gospel.

Spiritual imprisonment can happen at any time, but we know there is a due time for release. There was a time for Peter to be released as the church continued to intercede, the Lord sent His angels to release him. When it was time for Paul and Silas to be released as they prayed and praised God, the foundations were shaken by the Holy Ghost and they were released forcefully.

Samson made a lot of mistakes, but when it was time for him to get out, when he prayed, the Holy Ghost came upon him again and he was released, glory to God! On many different occasions he escaped imprisonment, he escaped the snare. That is the grace and mercy of God that speaks for those in prison.

Jesus was also locked up and he was thrown into prison, even Jesus our Lord was in prison! The process of the cross involved His imprisonment. So, you can see whether a person is watchful or not watchful, things like this can happen.

We also have those who have been imprisoned physically. They've been put into federal penitentiaries and jail houses for crimes they didn't commit. Today we're going to ask for justice for both spiritual and physical imprisonments. We want to ask for justice and that the voice of God would resound. We ask for this verdict because His verdict overrides every other verdict, even the verdict of the natural judges. We know the verdict of the Lord God shall indeed override every verdict a man can think of, and this day we trust Him to release His verdict, release His angels, and release the power of the Holy Ghost into these places spiritually and physically. We decree a release of many and multitudes out of prison houses! We decree breakthroughs! We decree a breaking through and breaking forth in the name of Jesus! We decree that foundations will shake in the name of Jesus! We decree a release this day! Would you pray with me?

Prayer:

Father, in the name of Jesus, we thank You, because You are the God of justice and we can trust You to release men and women out of prison houses, both physically and spiritually. Lord God, Joseph was accused for a crime he didn't commit, but when it was time and when the book of remembrance was opened, that day, You called his name and called him out of that prison house. This day we decree the same thing oh God, that many are coming out of everywhere they have been falsely accused, both physically and spiritually!

We declare they are coming out in the name of Jesus! Any form of unforgiveness, bitterness or offense in our heart that the enemy is using to keep us bound, Lord, this day we decree that we release everyone who hurt us, offended us, or wounded us. We release them and we also forgive them, and we forgive ourselves. We decree that unforgiveness will not keep us bound, bitterness and offenses will not keep us bound, and it will not be that which the enemy will use to bring us into captivity!

This day we release them from our heart, we release them from our souls, we decree that just like a bird, they are released from us this day in the name of Jesus! We decree that by the mercies of God and by the hand of God they are released from our hearts. We decree that they will also release us from their hearts. Anyone who is holding us in their hearts or anyone that's holding us by any reason, we decree this day Father, that they release us from their hearts in the name of Jesus!

I speak life to anyone reading this or speaking these words. I speak life to anyone that the enemy has shown how to shut out your heart from giving love or forgiveness, in the name of Jesus! I pray this day by the mercy of God, that every hold is broken, in the name of Jesus. Light shines and darkness comprehended it not (John 1:5). In the name of Jesus, I pray that your eyes can see that your heart is flooded with light!

In any way, anyone reading or speaking these words who has chained people and locked them up in your heart and refused to let go, I declare the mercy of God, for this is the love of God that while we were yet sinners Christ died for us (Romans 5:8). I pray your eyes be opened to see the finished work of Jesus Christ and how much love He has poured out to you. I pray that you would receive that love today in the name of Jesus Christ of Nazareth!

I pray you begin to release them now whoever has offended you, whoever has molested you, whoever has accused you in any way, shape, or form, or whoever has stolen from you. I pray right now through the grace of God, that is available in Jesus Christ, that your heart is open to receive in the name of Jesus Christ of Nazareth!

Every form or fashion of imprisonment that has taken place, even through accusations and pointing of the finger, and every word of accusation declared over you, every curse word, every lie, and every gathering together against the child of God, Lord, as they have released everyone who has offended them and everyone who has accused them, out of their heart, right now I declare every such curse words and accusations are now broken completely in the name of Jesus! The fetters are broken completely in the name of Jesus!

The agendas are destroyed by the anointing in the name of Jesus! I declare your liberty now from every spiritual imprisonment in the name of Jesus!

Anywhere you've been thrown into because of jealousy and envy, may the mercy and love of God bring you out and may He vindicate you in the name of Jesus! I declare justice on your behalf! May the Lord justify you, may He indeed! He who justifies the poor in the name of Jesus, may the Lord indeed be your voice!

May He speak for you in the night hour! May He speak for you in secret places when they accuse you, speak lies about you, speak incantations, false words or words of darkness and divination over you, in the name of Jesus!

May the Lord be your Defense! May the Lord be your Rearguard and Reward! May the Lord be your voice in the name of Jesus! Therefore, every accusation, every word curse, every fiery dart shot at you, because of jealousy or envy, in the name of Jesus, I declare right now your liberty! I declare right now your freedom! Every dart shot at you of betrayal, the accuser of the brethren, guarded sons and daughters of Belial that speak lies against you to accuse you in the night hour and accuse you in the dark places, in the name of Jesus Christ, let the agenda break! Let the operation be destroyed now in the name of Jesus!

For God shall indeed now lift you up by His mighty hand, in the name of Jesus! Whatever pits they have dug for you, anything they have proposed in their heart, principalities and powers that have gathered together to place you in the pit where there is no water, and they are waiting for you to die, and they are waiting for you to be completely taken out; the devil is a liar in the name of Jesus!

I declare right now that the voice of Jesus sounds like many waters even into the dark regions, let His voice lift you up out of that pit right now in the name of Jesus (Revelation 1:15)! Now I declare judgment, that the justice of the Lord reigns, may His voice resound on your behalf! Let justice reign! Let justice reign in the name of Jesus!

I declare every work of the devil and every agenda of wickedness that keeps you in spiritual imprisonment, every yoke of witchcraft, every yoke of the devil, every yoke to keep you bound in chains, to keep you bowed and barred from where you are to be, in the name of Jesus, I declare now that justice reigns! Let the verdict be served by the Most High God by the reason of the finished work of Jesus Christ! I declare your liberty and I declare you are coming out of that place, in the name of Jesus!

Any word curses or any accusations from the pit of hell, may the Lord dissolve them all now by the blood of Jesus in Jesus name! Let the verdict be served in the name of Jesus!

Hebrews 13:3 says, "Remember the prisoners as if chained with them—those who are mistreated—since you yourselves are in the body also." We pray right now remembering every single one who is bound.

We declare this day even those in physical prison houses, federal penitentiaries, and jail houses, Lord, we know that it is your purpose and plan to give them the light of the gospel of Jesus, therefore we ask for justice this day according to the will of God and according to the standard of God.

Any word curses or accusations that have put people in prison for crimes they didn't commit, we declare this day that you are set free by the verdict of the Most High God in the name of Jesus! We declare the finished work of Christ is speaking for you!

Worry not and fret not! Just as a Joseph was accused for a crime he didn't commit, I've come to announce to someone this day in the name of Jesus the King, the Lord of lords will call for you also! He will call your name; He will call you out of that prison and jail house and He will crown you in the name of Jesus! May He exalt you, may He promote you just as he did for Joseph, for your promotion also is around the corner!

I prophesy to someone today that life will spring forth according to Isaiah 43:19 out of this accusation that has put you in prison in the name of Jesus! We declare this day that prison houses are receiving the verdict of the Lord! Physical prisons and spiritual prisons, we declare the verdict of the Lord in these places in the name of Jesus! We declare your liberty in the name of Jesus and that the light of the gospel is shining!

We declare that the standard is the rule of the Lord God Almighty! Therefore, even to those who are blind and in prison houses, we declare that the light of the gospel is shining! We declare that your soul is saved unto the Lord Jesus Christ, in the name of Jesus!

Every plot and agenda released against you and God's people to put them in prison, in the name of Jesus, this day let the verdict of the Lord be heard! For in Him we trust! Father we trust You, we trust Your word and Your verdict! We trust that You're a righteous Judge, therefore we declare justice is served oh God! For You do not rejoice in unrighteousness or injustice! We declare that Heaven has come down upon the earth this day and justice is served, in the name of Jesus!

Any injustice that has kept anyone in prison both spiritually and physically, this day in the name of Jesus, we declare your release by the verdict of the Lord, in the name of Jesus! Psalm 69:33 says, "For the LORD hears the poor, And does not despise His prisoners." We declare now, the cloak of the Lord is coming upon you wherever you are! The cloak of comfort, the cloak of peace, all over your heart in the name of Jesus! Acts 12:5 says, "Peter was therefore kept in prison, but constant prayer was offered to God for him by the church."

We know he was released by a supernatural order. In the same way we declare the angels of the living God are released into the prison houses both physical and spiritual, in the name of Jesus! For a supernatural order, for the release, and for the verdict to be executed in whatever way the Father wills! We declare it is happening again! If it happened before, it's happening again, in the name of Jesus, for we serve a God of yesterday, today, and forever (Hebrews 13:8).

Let the angels of the living God sweep into the prison houses and begin to execute a supernatural order! We declare the chains are falling off, the chains that have bound are falling off, in the name of Jesus! Let them fall off now, in the name of Jesus!

Any imprisonment that has happened by conspiracy both physical and spiritual, every evil plot and evil counsel, we decree your release by the mandate of Jehovah! The conspiracies and confederacies have come to naught in the name of Jesus! They are now broken, and they are exposed in the name of Jesus! By the mandate of Jesus Christ of Nazareth, we decree your release to the glory of God, in the name of Jesus!

In any way our youth or our children have been ensnared to be put in prison and their destinies truncated, we decree this day, the devil lied, and the devil is defeated in his plan toward our children and our youth! His plans are dissolved by the blood of Jesus! We decree a release today! We decree eyes are open and the light has shown in their heart and the light has shown in their darkness, in the name of Jesus! Be released, in the name of Jesus! Be released from any imprisonment. The shackles and the chains are broken, in the name of Jesus! The chains are falling off, glory to God! The Holy Spirit is leading you out of every prison house, in the name of Jesus! By a supernatural decree and order in the name of Jesus!

Father, we thank You! I've come to announce to someone today, you are entering your new season! You're entering a new season; out with the old and in with the new! Here comes a new season for you, in the name of Jesus!

Just as David announced, "My soul is escaped as a bird," I prophesy that to your soul! I prophesy that to you also! Your soul has escaped, glory to God! By the hand of God, the cage is broken, in the name of Jesus! You are breaking out and you are breaking forth! Here comes your breakthrough, in the name of Jesus! Be released, in the name of Jesus! Be released into your new season, in the name of Jesus! We declare a shift, in Jesus name and in the atmosphere, in the name of Jesus!

Lord we thank You! We thank You, Lord God for releasing Your children out of the prison, both physically and spiritually! We thank You for releasing them out of the prison, in the name of Jesus!

We declare the hour has come just as it came for Paul and Silas, just as it came for Peter, just as it came for Joseph, for David and Mordecai! We declare the book of remembrance is opened, in the name of Jesus! It is so, amen! Amen! Amen! Thank you, God. We give You all the praise, all the glory, and all the honor, in Jesus name we have prayed, amen!

Additional Information

We send books into prisons free of charge!

To order a book for your loved one that's incarcerated please visit the website or write to the address below. Prior to making your request please check with the unit to ensure books can be sent directly from Amazon to the person, as each state and unit is different. All books are sent in paperback form.

Be sure to include the following:

- Person's name
- Offender ID#
- Address of unit (cell/bunk # if required by their unit)

Website: www.purchasedinnocence.com
Email: info@purchasedinnocence.com
Phone: (512) 956-8444
Address:
10650 Culebra Rd #104-138
San Antonio, TX 78251

We receive mail from correctional facilities at the address listed above. Please write to us and share how this book has impacted you or to share your own testimony.

If this book has made an impact in your life or to share your own testimony, please write to me at the email or address above.

Made in United States
Troutdale, OR
07/16/2023